D0593704

WITHDRAWN FROM MONROE COLLEGE LIBRARY

For James and Gillian

For James and Gillian

JIM GILL'S NEW YORK

James F. Gill

Fordham University Press
New York • 2003

KF
373
.G56
A3
2003

Copyright © 2003 by James F. Gill

All rights reserved. No part of this publication may be reproduced, stored in a retrieval system, or transmitted in any form or by any means—electronic, mechanical, photocopy, recording, or any other—except for brief quotations in printed reviews, without the prior permission of the publisher.

All photographs are from the author's collection.

Library of Congress Cataloging-in-Publication Data

Gill, James F., 1931–
    For James and Gillian : Jim Gill's New York /
James F. Gill.—1st ed.
      p.   cm.
    Includes index.
    ISBN 0-8232-2236-5 (alk. paper)
    1. Gill, James F., 1931– 2. Lawyers—New York
(State)—New York—Biography. I. Title.
    KF373.G56 A3   2003
    340′.092—dc21   2002013576

Printed in the United States of America
03   04   05   06   07   5   4   3   2   1
First Edition

CONTENTS

PREFACE

I'VE BEEN FORTUNATE indeed. I've had the benefit of magnificent parents, a loving grandfather who was my first pal, a totally devoted aunt who took me in and raised me when my mother died, an incredibly generous and supportive uncle, and other caring relatives as well.

I was afforded an education that I would not exchange for any other in the world, and I have experienced the great joy and consolation that the Roman Catholic faith affords.

I've been with my law firm for more than thirty-eight years. I've had the privilege of enormously gifted and delightful law partners and a talented secretary who served me for more than thirty-five years. I've had the opportunity, the pleasure, and the satisfaction of serving my church, my city, my state, and my nation in meaningful ways.

I've been blessed with a host of friends, tested and true over the years, that are without equal.

But my greatest treasures are the members of my immediate family: Jackie, my wife of forty-three years; my children, Patrick, Rose, and Dennis; my son-in-law, Francis James Hearn Jr.; my grandson, Francis James Hearn III (known as James in deference to his maternal grandfather—me); and my granddaughter, Gillian Rose Hearn. This book is dedicated to all of them.

I had never considered writing a book until the arrivals of our grandchildren. As I approached my seventy-first birthday, I decided to write this book for them and any additional grandchildren with whom we may be blessed. I wanted James and Gillian to know my history, my beliefs, my accomplishments, and the way I've conducted my life. And I wanted them to get it directly from *me*.

I

EARLY YEARS

1

Waterbury and a Different Era

I WAS BORN on September 4, 1931, at St. Mary's Hospital in Waterbury, Connecticut, a vibrant, surging manufacturing hub in the Naugatuck Valley. My family lived in a three-family house, like everybody else we knew. Usually the owner would occupy the first floor, and the cellar would be subdivided among the three families. The source of heat was coal, which was delivered by men who carried it in huge sacks on their backs. They would dump the coal onto a ramp that led from the cellar window to a bin next to the furnace. The ashes from the burned coal were frequently used to melt snow and ice on sidewalks during the winter. There was no air-conditioning—except at the movies. Food was kept cold in iceboxes, and ice men would deliver massive blocks of ice which they carried on their backs, like the coal men. They used huge tongs and large slabs of leather that insulated their backs from the intense cold.

There were trolleys and horse-drawn milk wagons. Bottles of milk were delivered to our door every other day, and we would leave our empty bottles for the milkman to retrieve. It was the general belief that the consumption of enormous quantities of whole milk (there was no other kind then) was essential for the good health of a growing child. Given what we know today, and the enormous amount of milk I was forced to drink, I'm lucky to have survived childhood! In those days, there were three sit-down meals a day: breakfast, lunch, and dinner. Everyone was expected to attend and to be on time. I believe that the loss of that great American tradition has been seriously harmful to family life.

When a family member became ill with something beyond the common cold, the doctor would be called, and he would come to the house carrying a large black bag.

Our fathers all worked in the factories in Waterbury. For us Roman Catholics, the center of all activity was our parish, which in my case was St. Margaret's, on Willow Street. As a matter of fact, you were frequently identified by the parish to which you belonged (for example, "Joe Murphy from Sacred Heart"). All my family and everyone I knew were enrolled Democrats and Roman Catholics. (I still am and always will be.) There were the Irish, the Italians, the Germans, the Poles, and the Lithuanians, who, by and large, lived in separate sections of the city. While Waterbury's factories were highly unionized, most workers believed in "a good day's work for a good day's pay," and the tremendous work ethic of our local work force was undoubtedly our greatest asset. The only women who worked were single women who did office work.

We referred to Waterbury as "the brass center of the world" and, to a lesser extent, "the clock center of the world"— Switzerland notwithstanding. The Benrus Watch Company, the Lux Clock Manufacturing Company, and Timex were all located in the area, and Waterburians also boasted of companies like Scoville Manufacturing Company (where my father worked as a machinist), the E. J. Manville Machine Company, the American Mills Company, the Waterbury Battery Company, the Waterbury Jewel Company, and the American Brass Company. It was said that Waterbury had produced all the brass casings for the shells used during World War I. The city's motto was: "Waterbury has something on everybody." (Frequently it was the grippers on your shorts! Remember those?)

And the moral climate was drastically different for what it is today. Divorce was almost unheard of, adultery was a major scandal, and premarital sex was rare. We took honesty, integrity, and truth-telling for granted. There were *no* drugs. The closest we came to smoking marijuana was smoking dried corn silk. (Most of us got sick on the first try and never did it again.) Alcohol and cigarettes were prevalent, however, among adult males.

My mother's maiden name was Rose Anne Shanahan. She was the eldest of her siblings; the others were my aunt Nell, my uncle John, my uncle Eddie, my uncle Tom, and my uncle Dennis. Their father, John Shanahan, worked in a factory and developed the seamless boiler, for which he received no additional remuneration and very little recognition.

His father, my great-grandfather William Shanahan, joined the

Connecticut Volunteers during the Civil War. He was wounded during the Battle of the Wilderness and was later imprisoned at Libbey Prison in Richmond, Virginia. Family folklore has it that at one point during the Battle of the Wilderness, his commanding officer was in a desperate situation and anxiously asked, "Is Shanahan here?" When the answer came back in the affirmative, he responded: "Then let the battle go on!" While the story seems like a bit of a stretch, I believed every bit of it when I was a kid—and I still do!

My grandmother Shanahan's maiden name was Julia Curran. She died at a relatively young age, and my aunt Nell took over the care of the Shanahan household. My aunt Nell was a dedicated, devoted, loyal and loving homemaker.

My mother was handsome and bright, and possessed a delightful sense of humor as well as an interest in the finer things in life. My daughter, Rose, is named after my mother and has a lot of her stuff.

My father was also the oldest child in his family. He had to leave school after the sixth grade to help support his brothers and sisters. My favorite aunt on my father's side was my aunt Marcy, a short, stocky woman who could curse up a blue streak. She married Bill Neville, a fine man who was a big, strapping, two-fisted, hard-drinking truck driver. I remember being at my aunt Marcy's house on one occasion when Neville came home after having had too much to drink. As soon as he opened the door, Aunt Marcy greeted him with a right cross to the jaw—and called him everything under the sun. He blinked and headed immediately for the bedroom, with Marcy pummeling and cursing him every inch of the way. She had a heart of gold—but she didn't like drinking, and Neville was scared to death of her! I knew instinctively that she loved me—and I loved her back.

My uncle Tom Gill founded a tool-and-die company in Waterbury and did well, as did my uncle Ed Gill, who was in the milk business. I had two aunts on my father's side beside my aunt Marcy, my aunt Ann and my aunt Helen, both of whom were registered nurses. (I never met my grandparents on the Gill side, and there was never any conversation about them to which I was privy.) My mother died when I was four. Shortly before she died, she asked Aunt Nell to take care of me, since my father, of course, had to work. My aunt Nell adored my mother and readily agreed. Her husband, John Golden, was a draftsman at the Plume and Atwood Factory. Soon after Aunt Nell took me in, they had a child, my cousin Jack, whom I regard as not merely a cousin but my brother. My aunt Nell was a magnificent woman. In addition to being a superb homemaker, she was an American history buff and very much into the politics of the day. She was also a fierce defender of all of her relatives—right or wrong. I could not have had a better mother, and I would not trade my boyhood for the boyhood of anybody else in the world.

In those days, there were no old age "homes" except state institutions. No one was ever "put away," and it was common for a family to include a grandparent, a widowed or spinster aunt, a single uncle, or a child with a lifelong illness. My grandfather lived with us, and I spent my early years with him on virtually a daily basis. We had great fun together and became known in the neighborhood as "the old man and the kid."

I remember setting up a lemonade stand with some of my friends at the corner of Plaza and Elmwood Avenues one hot summer day—with my grandfather looking on, far in the background. A newspaper reporter appeared on the scene, and the next day a picture of me and my friends appeared in the local paper. I loved the publicity—even then!

My grandfather had a profound impact on my development. He taught me basic and fundamental principles of: working 10 percent harder than your toughest competitor; never forgetting to say thank you;[1] and always being kind and considerate of other people—*all* people. He also bought me a piggy bank and urged me to save money. That was the only lesson that didn't take. I never had any money growing up, and I've never been interested in accumulating it for its own sake. I've always felt that money was something you needed to take care of your family's basic needs, a few luxuries, and to educate your kids.

My grandfather and I were the only two Waterburians that I knew of who rooted for the Brooklyn Dodgers. Most Waterburi-

---

[1] To this day I am resentful of those who fail to express thanks when they should.

Riding one of my polo ponies in Waterbury.

ans were Yankees fans. My friends and I spent hours, days, weeks in heated arguments over which team was better. Each position was analyzed closely. Pee Wee Reese was compared against Scooter Rizzutto; Mickey Owen against Bill Dickey; Billy Herman against Joe Gordon; Dixie Walker, Pete Reiser and Ducky Medwick against Joe DiMaggio, Tommy Henrick, and Charlie Keller; Dolph Camilli against Buddy Hassett; Cookie Lavagetto against Red Rolfe. It wasn't easy for me—the statistics from the *Sporting News* and the win/loss records of the respective teams were somewhat daunting—but I never gave up. And I never conceded a thing! I still say those Dodgers were the better team!

Once a year, my grandfather would take me to Ebbets Field for a Dodgers game, and it was the treat of the year. We would get there before the gates opened and we wouldn't leave until the final out—no matter what. What a wonderful ballfield it was—it was like being in heaven! One year, my uncle Tom got us front-row, field-level box seats. We were practically on the field! The front-row seats weren't bolted down, so you could move them to suit your convenience. I would move my seat to the front of the box, grab the rail, and dangle my forearms on the chicken wire. Ducky Medwick hit a foul ball into that chicken wire, and the force of it knocked me off my seat. Although I wasn't hurt at all, the people from the Dodgers organization took me into their dugout and put me on the training table—not because they were afraid of a lawsuit, but because that's the way it was! It really was a different era. I remember how Whitlow Wyatt, a twenty-game winner and the Dodger's ace pitcher that season, gave my right arm a rubdown. It was the biggest thrill of my life. I didn't wash that arm for weeks! By the way, the first outfield walls to be padded were those in Ebbets Field, to protect Pete Reiser. He was fearless and would try to go through walls in order to catch fly balls! Unfortunately, the wall usually won, and Reiser would wind up in the hospital.

When I was a boy, baseball was *everything*. During the summer months when school was out, we would go out immediately after breakfast and play ball, come home for lunch, go back out and play until dinner, and then go back out after dinner until it got too dark to see the ball! I was captain of St. Margaret's baseball team and played shortstop. We had great uniforms but we didn't win many games. I could field, throw, and run, but I was a lousy

John W. Shanahan: "Gramp."

hitter—a very serious shortcoming. But I played hard—and I played to win. There is no other way. I know that some Little League officials say winning is not important, but they are seriously misguided. And the parents of Little Leaguers should have absolutely no say about the conduct of the game. Otherwise the great basic lessons of competition, sportsmanship, and merit, which Little League baseball has the potential to offer, will be needlessly undermined.

We had baseball cards that cost a penny apiece and came with a delicious slab of pink bubble gum. Those cards were bought, collected, traded, and won in two types of competition: "Closest to the Wall" and "Flips on Top." I had a great collection that included almost every player who ever played for the Dodgers.

Our other sources of recreation were the radio and the movies. The radio offered programs like *The Inner Sanctum Mysteries; Sam Spade, Detective; The Shadow; The Green Hornet; I Love a Mystery; Jack Armstrong, the All American Boy; Nick Carter, Master Detective; Amos 'n' Andy; Jack Benny; Fred Allen; Edgar Bergen and Charlie McCarthy; Fibber McGee and Molly;* and *Ozzie and Harriet.* They were wonderful programs, and everyone who had a radio listened to them. Sometimes neighbors who didn't have a radio would join us—that's the way it was.

On Saturday afternoons, we went to the movies. For eleven cents, you got the main feature plus a second movie (of substantially lesser quality), the "Movietone News," cartoons, and a serial. (The serial I remember most fondly was *The Lone Ranger,* with his ever-faithful companion Tonto, about whom there have been too many cruel jokes! Tonto was a good man and deserved better!) We would spend almost all of every Saturday in a theater. Then we would go to White Castle for a hamburger. Those were the most delicious hamburgers I ever ate in my life—although I doubt they were any better than the hamburgers of today.

My favorite movies of the day were *The Maltese Falcon, Boys Town, Key Largo, Dracula, Casablanca, Frankenstein, Angels with Dirty Faces, The Road to Mandalay, The Wolf Man, Going My Way, Jekyll and Hyde, The Bells of St. Mary's, White Heat,* and all the comedies with the Bowery Boys, Abbott and Costello, the Three Stooges, Mickey Rooney (as Henry Aldrich), and the Marx Brothers.

It was the era of the big bands: Glenn Miller, Tommy Dorsey, Duke Ellington, Harry James, Jimmy Dorsey, Benny Goodman. The popular artists of the day were the Mills Brothers ("Up the Lazy River"), Fats Waller ("The Joint Is Jumping"), Bunny Barrigan ("I Can't Get Started with You"), Frankie Carle ("Sunset Serenade"), Vaughan Monroe ("Racing with the Moon"), Ella Fitzgerald ("A Tisket, A Tasket"), Bing Crosby ("White Christmas"), and that skinny kid by the name of Frank Sinatra, who titillated and traumatized teenage girls across America with songs—the titles of which I can't remember!

Another great treat was reading the funny papers on Sundays— "Dick Tracy," "Terry and the Pirates," "Smiling Jack," "Joe Palooka," "Little Orphan Annie," "Dagwood," "Gasoline Alley," "Flash Gordon." Then, of course, there were the comic books, like *Superman, Captain Marvel, Batman,* and the "Classic Comics" series, which some of us used for book reports.

The great summer treat in Waterbury was the arrival of the Ringling Brothers and Barnum & Bailey Circus. The circus would hire local kids to help put up the tents and the bleachers, and for other odd jobs—and I reported for duty. The first couple of years, I was turned down because I was too small. But eventually they hired me. The pay was a meal we called "scrapple," which consisted of scrambled eggs with ham and other mysterious ingredients—plus a ticket to one of the performances. I have a vague recollection that they used elephants in some way to put the tents up, but I'm not sure how . . .

I loved the circus, and I still do. The problem is that at my age, I'm somewhat hesitant about going alone, lest I get arrested—so I'm anxiously awaiting the day when I can bring James and Gillian!

When I was growing up, the dread fear of polio, or infantile paralysis, used to cast a pall over every summer. Every year, it took its toll. One year, it claimed one of the children attending St. Margaret's, and we were all deeply saddened and scared.

Every year, on the "Movietone News," President Roosevelt, himself a polio victim, would introduce the infantile paralysis poster child in connection with the March of Dimes fundraising drive. The child was always breathtakingly beautiful and smiling—but usually weighted down with heavy leg braces and dependent upon crutches. It was commonly thought that mosquitoes were carriers of polio, and accordingly I was strictly forbidden from going to any of the many lakes in the Waterbury area, for swimming or any other reason, during the summer. Think of the relief that Jonas Salk brought to millions of children and their parents when he developed the polio vaccine. What an incredible contribution to humankind!

In the wintertime, there was sledding and ice-skating. Waterbury had a lot of hills and used to get a great deal of snow. We would slide down those hills on our Flexible Flyers, making efforts along the way to "ditch" each other—that is to say, run the other person's sled into the gutter. I remember that a later model of the Flexible Flyer had a rounded runner in the rear that looked sharp but rendered that sled very susceptible to "ditching." You could grab the runner from behind and turn the sled into a ditch with ease. The hills where I lived were especially steep and long, and sledding was somewhat dangerous. There weren't many cars back then, but we had some close calls. And I remember sledding right through the legs of a horse that was attached to a milk wagon, which scared the hell out of me. Fortunately, the horse was not moving and apparently unaware of my intrusion. I can't remember anyone being seriously injured as a result of sledding—and it was spectacular fun!

Ice-skating at Fulton Park was the other winter sport. I wasn't very good at it—my favorite part was sitting around the huge fireplace that was always crackling to keep the skaters warm, and drinking hot cocoa. My sons, Patrick and Dennis, both played ice hockey during their boyhoods, and they ridicule me because I wasn't a skater as a boy. I tell them that the ankle supports that they were able to take advantage of—were not available to me!

I had a number of jobs when I was in grammar school. I was an altar boy. The Mass was said in Latin. That wasn't my problem. I had learned the Latin quickly and knew it better than most. My problem was maintaining my composure at the altar. When I was paired with certain friends, we would get hysterical for no reason at all. The pain of trying to maintain composure was nothing short of excruciating. To this day, I don't know why we did that, particularly in view of the solemnity of the Mass—and the severity of the punishment that would have been imposed had we been caught! Fortunately, under the Church liturgy of the day, the priest had his back to the congregation most of the time, and we altar boys knelt behind the priest with our backs to the congregation as well!

I also had a job delivering the Waterbury *Republican American* seven days a week. I'd pick up my papers at the corner of Plaza Avenue and Willow Street before sunrise and fold them into what we called "scalers"—so we could "scale" them onto the porches of the customers. (Every house had a porch.) But the Sunday paper was very thick and didn't lend itself to being made into a scaler. So on Sunday mornings I would use a wagon to deliver the papers, and it was much more difficult and time-consuming. I delivered the papers in all weather, snow, sleet or rain—just like the postman. My customers appreciated the service, particularly in inclement weather, and would sometimes reward me with a generous tip.

In the wintertime, I shoveled snow for neighbors. I had a list of regular customers.

In the late summer and early fall, I would pitch hay. That is, I would go to the various farms in the areas around Waterbury and help get the hay into the barn for the winter season. I was usually the guy up in the barn receiving the hay from below and stacking it. The dust was almost blinding, and I would be sneezing incessantly. It paid well, but it led to a serious and persistent case of hay fever in later years.

From kindergarten through eighth grade, I went to St. Margaret's, and I had nuns for teachers in seven of the nine years. Those nuns were precious and played an extraordinarily important role in the development of the children they taught! The Sisters of Mercy, who taught at St. Margaret's, showed us precious little mercy. Misbehavior in the classroom was never tolerated. The principal was Sister Mary Alberta, and if you were sent to her, it was a very serious bit of business—both at school and at home. Each day began with a prayer and The Pledge of Allegiance. Every day ended with a prayer. We studied reading, writing (the Palmer method), arithmetic, spelling, geography, history, science, music, art, and religion. We had homework every night, a test in some subject almost every day, final examinations, and report cards. If you didn't meet the requirements, you were kept back. There was *no* "social promotion" to *any* grade. School started at 8:30 A.M. and got out at 3:30 P.M., with an hour out for lunch at home. Everyone had to be there on time. There was no PTA, and the nuns couldn't have cared less about what the parents said or thought! Playing in the playground (there was one for the boys and another for the girls) before school and during recess was great fun. Occasionally a severe snowstorm would cause school to be called off, which made for enormous joy, snow forts, and snowball fights.

On Saturday afternoons at four-thirty, everyone went to confession, whether you needed to or not. And every Sunday morning at eight-thirty, we attended Mass with our classmates, under the watchful eye of our teacher. All of the holy days were celebrated in very special and inspiring ways. The Catholic religion was taught strictly from the Baltimore Catechism. We were told precisely what was right, what was wrong, what we could do, what we couldn't do, and what the respective rewards and punishments would be. (I would urge our Catholic parochial schools to go back to the Baltimore Catechism, or its equivalent.)

In retrospect, I realize that in the eighth grade I *may* have had impure thoughts about Margaret Dickinson, Rose Mary Bergen, Nancy Meehan, Elaine Nagle, and maybe four or five others. *But I'm not sure.* That may explain why I didn't confess them! Stark terror is another explanation.

I was a good student at St. Margaret's and generally behaved well, but I got into trouble from time to time. Probably the most serious thing I did was getting together with some of my cohorts one Halloween night and destroying a number of marble planters that belonged to people who were mean and nasty and had turned us away abruptly when we had come to their doors earlier in quest of candy. The planters were valuable, and we got caught. Our parents made restitution, and I got a licking. But the police didn't make any permanent record—they had that kind of discretion.

On another occasion, a friend and I were playing with matches and accidently set the Lincoln Street Woods on fire. We did our best to put it out, but before we knew it, the flames were heading towards Weinstein's garages on Plaza Avenue. I was scared. I ran as fast as I could to the local firehouse and told the firemen that the Lincoln Street Woods were on fire and that I was worried that Weinstein's garages were going to catch fire. (I didn't tell them I had set the fire.) They went off to fight the fire, and I ran to my house and literally hid under the bed. I had never been so frightened! Thank God, Weinstein's garages were spared, and nothing bad happened to me. I think those firemen knew that I started the fire but decided to let me off because I reported it. That's the way it was.

One time I did something wrong (I can't recall what it was) and my grandfather was assigned the task of giving me a spanking. Spankings were very rare indeed, and I was afraid. He took me into his bedroom, closed the door, picked up a hairbrush, and placed me across his knees. He then patted me gently on the behind with the hairbrush and whispered, "Start crying"—which I did loudly and to my great joy. My Aunt Nell was convinced.

Probably the worst thing that happened to me as a kid was when my friends and I went on a camping trip to Waterville, just north of Waterbury. I went to the bathroom in the woods and wiped myself with poison ivy leaves! This turned out to be not only painful but enormously embarrassing. My rear end was encased in calamine lotion for weeks. Thank God, there were no permanent scars!

The big days were the holidays. My uncles John and Dennis were both single and would come to my aunt Nell's for Thanksgiving and Christmas and stay for several days. It was wonderful to be and talk with them. I learned a great deal from both of them, but particularly Uncle Den, who was exceptionally bright, well-read, and articulate. He had worked his way through the University of Notre Dame and was on one of the Rockne teams, not as a regular but as a "scrub." I frequently shared a room with him when he visited us, and every night before he went to bed he would kneel down and say his evening prayers. He served as a naval officer during World War II and eventually founded a successful construction company in Ellenville, New York. He died young, of a heart attack, in 1957. I was in the Marine Corps and took emergency leave to attend his wake and funeral in Ellenville. The wake was packed with a host of people who had been the beneficiaries of his unbelievable generosity, including a dwarf for whom Uncle Den had bought a trailer home. It became apparent during the wake that *all* of his good works had been done quietly and without fanfare. He was a magnificent man, and my son Dennis Francis is named after him.

Uncle Den was a very modest and shy man. He felt that his reticence had hurt him professionally, and he urged me to step up and be assertive. Those who know me will readily agree that I heeded his lesson—some might say too well!

In September 2000, I went to South Bend, Indiana, to attend a Notre Dame football game against Nebraska. I visited the dorms in which Uncle Den had lived and the chapel in which he had prayed. It was a moving experience, and I felt especially close to him throughout the entire day. I returned to South Bend in 2001 with my son Dennis, to see Notre Dame play Southern California. We were *both* immersed in the same nostalgia.

Uncle Tom left Waterbury to attend New York University's School of Commerce. While there, he worked as a messenger for the Federation Bank and Trust Company. He went on to become its chairman, president, and chief executive officer. During the Depression, he single-handedly saved that bank by imploring and convincing depositors not to withdraw their funds. He later expanded the company from a single-branch bank (at the corner of Thirty-fourth Street and Eighth Avenue) to a fifteen-branch bank with its headquarters at the Coliseum at Columbus Circle. He became the treasurer of the New York State Democratic Party. He was an incredible political fund-raiser and became extremely powerful in Democratic circles, not only in the city and state, but nationally. He was also a close friend of and the principal financial adviser and fund raiser for Francis Cardinal Spellman, the archbishop of New York. Uncle Tom was a mathematical wizard and a hardheaded businessman with an overpowering personality. He was enormously generous, and a man of unflinching integrity. He has always been my role model. While I have followed doggedly in his footsteps and may have exceeded him in certain respects, I will never be his equal—because I had *him* and he had *nobody.*

Dennis F. Shanahan during World War II: Uncle Den.

My Uncle Eddie also went to New York, where he put himself through New York University and became a CPA. He lived in Astoria, Queens, with his wife, my Aunt Julia, and his sons, my cousins Pat, Billy, and Johnny. My grandfather would frequently take me there on Sundays. Uncle Den would come over from Brooklyn, and Uncle John would come up from Philadelphia. My cousin Pat became a priest, my cousin Billy was a Naval Academy graduate and a career naval officer, and my cousin Johnny had a distinguished career as a reporter. All

Thomas J. Shanahan at the start of his career: Uncle Tom.

of them were recognized for their uncompromising honesty and integrity. My grandfather and I would come down on the train. Along the way, we would pass the Life Savers plant near Bridgeport—at which point my grandfather would give me a peppermint Life Saver. He would do the same on the return trip. Uncle Eddie would greet us at Grand Central Station, and we would go to Mass at St. Agnes Church on Forty-third Street before taking the subway out to Astoria. The subway ride was itself a major treat for me—although the herky-jerky left-hand turn just after Queens Plaza, on that very highly elevated track, always scared me a bit. Much of the adult conversation on those Sunday afternoons had to do with politics. Even at an early age, I found it of interest.

My Uncle John was sort of the character of the family. He served in World War I in France as a "top" sergeant in the Army. He also had put himself through Villanova University, where he earned an engineering degree. But he spent most of his life as a bookie in Philadelphia, in partnership with a man by the name of "Fatty." He regaled me and my cousins with all sorts of stories about World War I, as well as his adventures as a bookie—some of which, I'm sure, were true!

After my mother died, my father moved in with my aunt Marcy, and he and I often spent weekends together. On Sunday, December 7, 1941—Pearl Harbor Day—we went to the movies at the State Theater. I was in the fifth grade. When we emerged from the theater, there were bulletins, written in black crayon and wrapped around telephone polls, announcing the Japanese attack on Pearl Harbor. That was the first time I remember seeing my father in a state of anger. He used language I had never heard him use before!

He had been in the navy in World War I and served in the engine room of a destroyer that participated in action in the Atlantic. My father never told me about it, although I pressed him on the subject regularly. He wasn't into war stories.

On that Sunday afternoon, although well beyond the draft age, my father told me then and there that he was going back into the Navy to serve his country. And he did. He was given the rank of

My father's engine room crew during World War I. He is the last on the right in the front row.

chief machinist mate. There wasn't a moment of hesitation as to what he was going to do. His country had been attacked, and it was his job to defend it. It was as simple as that, and that's the way it was with most people during that era. Tom Brokaw's book entitled *The Greatest Generation* (1998) is on target.

The day after the bombing of Pearl Harbor, everyone in America gathered around their radios and listened to President Roosevelt's electrifying speech, which galvanized our nation for war:

> Yesterday, December 7, 1941—a date which will live in infamy—the United States of America was suddenly and deliberately attacked by naval and air forces of the Empire of Japan. . . . No matter how long it may take us to overcome this premeditated invasion, the American people in their righteous might will win through to absolute victory. . . . Hostilities exist. There is no blinking at the fact that our people, our territory, and our interests are in grave danger. With confidence in our armed forces—with the unbounding determination of our people—we will gain the inevitable triumph—so help us God.

My father was assigned as a senior instructor to train machinists at the Naval Training Station at the Great Lakes. He wasn't pleased with his assignment—he would rather have been aboard a fighting ship—but there was nothing he could do about it.

My grandfather died on December 27, 1941, at the age of seventy-two. I remember the wake, at Mulville's Funeral Parlor, and the funeral Mass, at St. Margaret's, and also remember feeling the full sting of the death of a loved one.

When a Catholic family is visited by death, there is only one meaningful consolation: the knowledge that your loved one is in Heaven with God and that someday you'll be reunited. I often wonder how those who do not believe in that concept are able to endure such overwhelming pain and suffering.

Father Cronin, then a curate at St. Margaret's, came to hear my grandfather's confession and administered the last rites. I overheard Father Cronin tell Aunt Nell that when he asked Gramp whether he wanted to go to confession, Gramp's answer was: "All I've done since my last confession was to call the Japs a bunch of bastards."

After the attack on Pearl Harbor, Waterbury's factories went into high gear. Women entered the workforce. Gasoline and food, especially meat, were strictly rationed. Waterbury was "blacked out" at night: I remember that the top half of all the automobile headlights were painted black, and all shades had to be drawn after dark. It was the belief that in the event of an air attack, the Naugatuck Valley would be a prime target, and understandably so—its factories were going like the hammers of hell in support of the war effort, just as they had during World War I. Young men of draft age who were rejected for whatever reason were looked down upon. It was wrong, but that's the way it was.

I remember my father coming home on leave with huge bags full of steaks, chops, and roast beef, precious commodities indeed during those days! He knew how to get around.

After the war, he returned to Scoville. If there had been a third world war, he'd have served in that one, too! He became a shop steward at Scoville and later a supervisor. He was big, rugged, handsome, and he loved to have a good time! He was street-savvy beyond words and had an explosive sense of humor. He was also the best-dressed factory worker you ever saw! But in retrospect, I don't think he ever got over the death of my mother. He was a fine father. At great sacrifice to himself, he put me through Holy Cross College and Fordham Law School. I was a good student at both schools, and he was very proud of my achievements. He posted my report cards on the union bulletin board at Scoville. That gave me increased incentive to do well.

He was a trade unionist from the top of his head to the tips of his toes. He instilled in me his thoughts and ideas on that subject at a very early age. I've never forgotten them—and I never will: the right to a just wage, the right to bargain collectively, and the right to strike.

He lost the tip of his right index finger in an industrial accident. When I was a boy, I was fascinated by that truncated finger, for reasons I still don't understand. But I never revealed that fascination.

At that point in Waterbury's history, most grammar school graduates were expected to complete high school, and I think most did.

But very few went on to college. Generally, high school was the end of the line academically. As graduation from St. Margaret's approached, I started thinking about going to Crosby, Waterbury's biggest and best high school, which all of the Shanahans had attended—until I received a telephone call from my Uncle Tom.

"Jimmy," said he, "For high school, you've got two choices: Cranwell Preparatory School [a Jesuit school in Lenox, Massachusetts] or LaSalle Military Academy [on Long Island, run by the Christian Brothers]. Which do you want?" It was as simple as that. He was the patriarch of the family, and my options were limited to one or the other. I said: "Uncle Tom, I'll go to Cranwell." To this day, I have no idea why I chose Cranwell, except maybe because it was closer to Waterbury. But I'm glad I did!

I've often worried about the sacrifices Uncle Tom and his wife, my aunt Anne, made to accommodate my four years at Cranwell. While Cranwell was clearly the turning point of my life, let me tell you that when I first arrived, I was not a happy Cranwellian. To begin with, I was perfectly happy with my life up to that point and I wanted it to continue. But that was not to be.

2

Cranwell and a Different World

I ARRIVED at Cranwell Preparatory School in September of 1945. Cranwell was an enormously expensive school. It was located in the foothills of the Berkshires and was breathtakingly beautiful. It was a former estate that a very wealthy man by the name of Cranwell had given to the Society of Jesus (the Jesuits). It had an eighteen-hole golf course, and cottages ringed several of the fairways. Juniors and seniors lived in the cottages. Freshmen lived in a magnificent building called St. Joseph's Hall, and sophomores lived in another building called Berkman's Hall, which was not as magnificent but very functional. Jesuit priests resided in all student living quarters. The main building was Cranwell Hall, where most of the Jesuits resided and which also housed the main chapel, the library, and the student dining room. There was a basketball gymnasium, a hockey rink, a football field, a baseball field, and tennis courts. The skiing, of course, was spectacular.

I was the only person in my freshman class who arrived by bus, and I soon realized I was probably the only student at Cranwell who didn't come from a wealthy family. And when I say wealthy, I mean wealthy, not just rich. One of my classmates was Roderick O'Neill, who was a member of the family that owned the General Tire Company, then a closely held family corporation. Another classmate was Mike Downey, the son of Morton Downey, the singer, and a substantial owner of the Coca-Cola Company. One of the eighth graders was Teddy Kennedy, the one who is now a senator from Massachusetts.

At first, I felt extremely uncomfortable in those circumstances, but I adapted to them relatively soon. Early in my freshman year, our football team played Fairfield Prep in Fairfield, Connecticut, and the Cranwell student body was transported to the game by bus. The route from Lenox, Massachusetts, to Fairfield went through the heart of Waterbury and probably its worst section— not that there were many good ones. One of my new classmates

Cranwell Hall.

got on my case about Waterbury being a "dump." Waterbury was my hometown and I felt duty-bound to defend it. I did a slow burn all the way from Waterbury to Fairfield, and when we got off the bus, I went after my heckler, whereupon he proceeded to beat the hell out of me.

My father had given me a boxing lesson that had served me well. He said to me, "When someone starts a fight with you, he usually won't know how to fight, and most probably will be right handed. What he'll do is throw a looping right hand punch at your head." He said that when that happened, I was to do the following: overcome my natural instinct to back away, and instead move forward; get my left arm inside of my attacker's oncoming right-hand punch; and hit him with my right fist flush in the face, with all of the force I could muster.

Unfortunately, my father did not tell me how to *start* a fight. When I got off the bus, I started the fight with a looping right hand punch to the head. My opponent slipped his left inside my right and hit me with full force in the face—and that was just about the end of the fight! Perhaps my opponent's father had given his son the same defensive lesson my father had given me!

In any event, we beat Fairfield Prep decisively, and it was a great day. And there was no heckling about Waterbury on the way back to Cranwell. When you stand up for what you believe in, most people will accord you respect.

I wasn't big enough to play varsity sports in a meaningful way, although I was on the basketball and baseball teams. I only got to play when we were ahead by a substantial margin. My most memorable experience as the second baseman for Cranwell was taking a throw from our catcher when an opposing player tried to steal second base. He came in with "feet up" and spiked me on the right shin. (In those days we wore metal cleats.) In response I hit him on the head with the baseball. He was called safe, and I was thrown out of the game for unsportsmanlike conduct. I still have a scar on my right shin—and I'm still glad I hit that son of a bitch on the head with the ball.

A normal day at Cranwell began with Mass and was followed by breakfast and classes until noon. After lunch, there were more classes, a couple of hours of recreation, and then a supervised study hall from 5:15 to 6:15 P.M. Next came supper and another supervised study hall from seven-thirty to nine-thirty. It was "lights out" at ten o'clock. On Saturday mornings, we had a half day of class.

A movie was shown in the gymnasium every Saturday night. You were permitted to see the movie only if you were not in "jug." Five demerits would put you in jug, and demerits were easily accumulated. You got demerits for missing or being late for class, Mass, or a meal. In winter, we were required to wear "hats, coats, and rubbers," and we were given demerits for failing to wear any one of those items. You could work off a demerit by raking leaves in the fall or shoveling snow in the winter. You got one demerit off for each hour of work.

Leaving the campus was as a very serious violation. Once, in our sophomore year, some of us caught a taxi into Pittsfield on a Saturday afternoon to see the movie *Blue Skies* starring Bing Crosby. The Jebbies (as we called the Jesuits) somehow got wind of our absence and came after us in their Jebmobiles. When we returned to the campus, we had our taxi driver let us out at a far end of the golf course, but just then a Jebmobile appeared on the scene. The penalty: thirty-five demerits (which meant, in effect, no more movies for the rest of the year), two days off our Easter vacation, and a letter home to the effect that another off-campus excursion would mean we were expelled. These guys didn't fool around, and we didn't go off the campus again.

My father gave me a small battery-operated Emerson radio before I went off for junior year, and I took it with me even though radios were strictly prohibited at Cranwell. I listened to it throughout my last two years at Cranwell and never got caught! My favorite program was broadcast on Friday night and opened as follows: "Bill Stern, the Colgate Shaving Man, is on the air." Stern would regale his audience with tales of highly sensational and unusual sporting feats. One of his programs concluded with a story about a man who swam across the Hudson River at its widest point—although he had no arms or legs! (Shortly thereafter, the program was canceled.)

At Cranwell we got four years of Latin, English, history, religion, math, and the sciences, and two years of a foreign language. Almost all the classes were taught by Jesuits. One of the most sought-after perks, and it was only available to juniors and seniors, was "room study," that is to say, permission to study in your room instead of the supervised study halls. In order to qualify for room study, you had to be on the Dean's List. I was on the Dean's List throughout junior and senior years, and what a joy it was not to have to go to study hall. I got 100 percent in two courses at Cranwell—Plane Geometry in my sophomore year and Trigonometry in my senior year. I liked getting 100 percent, and so did my father, Aunt Nell, and Uncle Tom!

In senior year, our basketball team was invited to participate in a statewide tournament at the Boston Garden. We lost 49–32 in the finals—but what a thrill for high school kids to play at the Boston Garden!

Many of my classmates were from the Boston area and rooted for the Boston Red Sox. I think it's fair to say that I was probably the *only* Brooklyn Dodger fan that ever attended Cranwell in all of its history. There were certainly no others when I was there! But I was used to being alone in the defense of my beloved Dodgers! It just so happened that in those days the Red Sox had one of the greatest teams in the history of baseball. In the outfield they had Ted Williams, Dom DiMaggio (the brother of Joe), and Al Zarrilla. The infield consisted of Rudy York, Bobby Doerr, Johnny Pesky and Vern Stephens. The catcher was Birdie Tebbetts, and the pitching aces were Mel Parnell and Dave "Boo" Ferriss (a Waterburian!). In 1946, my sophomore year, the Red Sox played the St. Louis Cardinals in the World Series. The Cardinals line-up included Stan Musial at first, Red Schoendienst at second, Slats Marion at shortstop, and Whitey Kurowski at third. The outfielders were Enos Slaughter, Terry Moore, and Harry Walker; the catcher was Joe Garagiola; and the pitching aces were Howie Pollet and Harry "the Cat" Brecheen.

The argument could be made that they were the two greatest teams that ever competed in a World Series. The Cardinals beat the Red Sox in the seventh game, by one run, when Harry Walker hit a double into the gap in the eighth inning and Enos Slaughter sprinted home from first base with the winning run!

My argument vis-à-vis my classmates who rooted for the Red Sox went something like this: The National League is vastly superior to the American League, as demonstrated by the outcome of the 1946 World Series. Moreover, the Dodgers are clearly a better team than the Cardinals (no basis). It therefore follows, as day follows night, that the Dodgers are a better team than the Red Sox. Some of my classmates from the Boston area had difficulty following the compelling logic of my argument. In any event, if you can't be rational, at least be bold!

The fact of the matter is that I've always had a soft spot in my heart for the Red Sox. Like the Dodgers, they have always been traditional rivals of the loathed and despised Yankees, and they haven't won a World Series since 1918. In addition, I've always admired Ted Williams, as a ballplayer and as a person. He served as a Marine Corps aviator during World War II and again during the Korean War. We'll never know what his statistics would have been without those huge gaps in his magnificent baseball career. When he passed away on July 5, 2002, at the age of eighty-three, the nation lost a great athlete and hero.

Jackie Robinson was one of the greatest that ever played the game. Branch Rickey had brought Robinson up from Montreal to play second base for the Dodgers—the first black man to play in the major leagues. When he got on base, electricity went through the ballpark because everyone knew that he would be stealing. He drove pitchers and catchers crazy—and he was most dangerous when he was on third base! He'd steal home in the blink of an eye—and often did! (Yogi Berra still maintains that Robinson was out at the plate when he stole home in the first game of the Dodgers-Yankees World Series in 1955.)

But it was a different era, and Robinson experienced terrible abuse because he was black—not only from opposing teams but from opposing fans, and indeed from some of his own teammates. But to my recollection, the Brooklyn Dodgers fans embraced him unreservedly—to their everlasting glory.

On May 14, 1947, at Crosley Field in Cincinnati, Pee Wee Reese, the revered captain of the Brooklyn Dodgers, provided America with one of the greatest moments in the annals of sports. On that day, the fans in Cincinnati started booing Robinson unmercifully—and it was clearly because he was black. It got so bad that the game was delayed—until Reese, a Southerner from Kentucky, left his position at shortstop, went over to Robinson at second base, and put his arm around Robinson's shoulders. The booing stopped immediately—and it never happened again!

I'm drifting. But a good writer will do that occasionally!

Cranwell was the turning point in my life. I was exposed to a spectacular classical education—and I learned how to study. I learned how to take care of myself. I was plunged into a very different world from the one I knew in Waterbury, and I experienced the ways and the lifestyles of the wealthy and the powerful. The people I met during my days at Cranwell were, trappings aside, basically the same as those I knew in Waterbury—no better, no worse. Ever since Cranwell, I have never been awed by wealth or power—not even a little bit. And I made friendships that endure to this day. You know, spending four years at a place like Cranwell is like going through a war—and you forge the same kind of friendships.

There's a lot to be said for boarding school. It's not for everyone, of course, but the independence that a young person can acquire as a result is something that merits serious consideration. It profited me enormously.

3

Holy Cross and Freedom

IN MY SENIOR YEAR at Cranwell, I applied to the University of Notre Dame and also to Holy Cross College. My application to Notre Dame was influenced by their strong civil-engineering program, my tremendous admiration for my Uncle Den, and the fact that he was in the construction business. I always thought it would be a great joy to work with him permanently. On the other hand, I truly enjoyed the classics, and many of my friends from Cranwell were going to Holy Cross, which was strong in the classics. Also, Holy Cross is located in Worcester, Massachusetts, which was closer to home than Notre Dame, which is in Indiana. And so I chose Holy Cross, with the understanding and indeed the blessing of my Uncle Den. It was the right choice.

At that time, Holy Cross was the premier Jesuit college in the country academically. It wasn't until many years later that other Jesuit colleges like Georgetown, Boston College, and Fordham University were able to close the academic gap somewhat. The reason they were able to do so had to do primarily with the prominent cities in which those schools are located—Washington, D.C., Boston, and New York City, respectively. In my time, students rarely ventured into the cities in which their colleges were located, since virtually all activities took place on campus. But that has changed, and now Washington, Boston, and New York have distinct advantages in attracting strong applicants and faculty.

I have advanced this thesis for many years and know that some of my friends who went to other Jesuit colleges are in sharp disagreement. I'm thinking particularly of my old and dear friend Paul Curran, who entered Georgetown the same year I entered Holy Cross. Paul objects whenever I refer to Holy Cross as the "Jesuit Mother School." He points out, correctly, that Georgetown was founded in 1789, the same year the United States Constitution took effect, and is the oldest Catholic university in the nation. Holy Cross was founded in 1843, some fifty-four years later. My answer to Paul is always the same: "There's a lot more to motherhood than mere longevity!" Recently I've been reminding Paul that President Clinton went to Georgetown, which really drives him crazy!

I traveled to Holy Cross in September of 1949, the same way I had traveled to Cranwell, namely, via public transportation. But at Holy Cross I wasn't the only one who did—the student body was much more diverse economically, and I think that was better for all of us. While the majority of students were from New England and the New York metropolitan area, there were representatives from all over the country. And for the *first* time in my life, I had fellow Brooklyn Dodgers rooters!

Holy Cross was a tough school, much like Cranwell. It was all male, and you couldn't even have your mother in your room! Attendance at *daily* Mass was compulsory. We had classes five and a half days a week (half a day on Saturday). It was "lights out" at ten o'clock every night except Saturday, when we could stay up until midnight. There were demerits and "jug," which at Holy Cross consisted of punching a clock every hour, on the hour, on Saturday nights.

There was a core curriculum of no-nonsense courses. In my first two years, I took Latin, Greek, math, science, English, history, religion, and Spanish. The last two years were dominated by philosophy and theology. The course I enjoyed the most was in logic, taught by a brilliant young Jesuit priest by the name of John P. Donnelly. I missed getting 100 percent in logic by a fraction of a point. In senior year the final exams in Philosophy were both written and oral.

But in comparison with Cranwell, Holy Cross was a country club: no study halls, no off-campus limitations, no mandatory attendance at meals (the cafeteria was open all day), and no "hats, coats, and rubbers"! We were even allowed to have radios!

Sports at Holy Cross were sensational. On Friday nights before football games, there was always a rally in the basement of St. Joseph's Chapel, and the place would rock! Almost every student went to every home football game, and many students went to the away games. We played teams like Syracuse, U-Mass, Harvard, Yale, and Dartmouth. It was a particular delight to travel to Dartmouth in the fall. Our traditional rival at that time was Boston College. Those were the days before Boston College went all out in sports, and before Holy Cross started drastically deemphasizing sports. The Holy Cross–Boston College football game was played on Thanksgiving Day, and it was the biggest football game in New England. It was played in Boston, either at Fenway Park or Braves Field. One of those BC pregame rallies got out of hand and spilled out of the basement of St. Joe's Chapel and onto the campus, after which virtually the entire student body marched from Holy Cross College into the center of Worcester, causing major traffic problems.

In my freshman year, the Holy Cross basketball team, under Bob Cousy's leadership, won its first twenty-six games in a row and was ranked No. 1 nationally by the Associated Press. Holy Cross lost to North Carolina State in the opening round of the NCAA tournament, but Cousy was named the nation's outstanding player by the Basketball Writers of America and, of course, an All-American.

Cousy was the most amazing player I have ever seen on a basketball court. When he got close to the basket, he would throw up shots—out of nowhere—and score without looking at the basket. He knew where it was instinctively. He was ambidextrous and an incredible play maker. He was the best dribbler I ever saw and invented the "around the back" dribble. In those days there was no time requirement to shoot on offense, and if Holy Cross was ahead in the closing minutes, Cousy would simply dribble Holy Cross to victory—and no one could do anything about it! He rarely looked at a fellow player to whom he was throwing a pass, and frequently it was behind the back. His passes were *always* on target! His speed and moves were breathtaking. While he was always a high scorer, he also had a tremendous number of assists. I think he was the best guard that ever played the game.

In my junior year, our basketball team, led by All-American Togo Palazzi, was invited to the National Invitational Tournament and defeated Seattle University in the opener before losing to Duquesne. That same year, our baseball team won the NCAA championship in Omaha, Nebraska.

In my senior year, our basketball team, led by All-Americans Togo Palazzi and Earle Markey, went to the NCAA tournament and beat Navy and Wake Forest before losing to Louisiana State University in the Eastern Regional Finals. (That year, Louisiana

State University had a center by the name of Bob Petitt!) And in that same year our football team went eight-and-two. Of special significance, however, was the fact that Boston College *never* beat Holy Cross in *any* sport during my senior year! I like to call it the year the Eagle never flew!

As I've said, Boston College has since gone all out to compete in sports at the highest level, whereas Holy Cross has deemphasized drastically. I regard both approaches as wrong. Boston College will never compete effectively with the nation's collegiate sports factories unless the Jesuits abandon academic achievement, which will never happen. Holy Cross, on the other hand, went too far in totally abandoning competitive athletics. I'm delighted that Holy Cross has recently started to become competitive again, particularly in basketball, and I hope that progress continues and intensifies.[1] Sports have always been and will always be a very important part of college life—as long as they are reasonably competitive! And they are of great importance to the alums who participated in or enjoyed varsity sports when they attended college. There's a middle ground, and both Holy Cross and Boston College should make that the target. I would love to see the old Holy Cross–Boston College sports rivalry restored someday!

Soon before I started at Holy Cross, my Aunt Nell, my cousin Jack Golden, and I moved to Stuyvesant Town in Manhattan. I took to Stuyvesant Town and New York City instantly. From that point on, my visits to Waterbury were primarily to see my father and my old boyhood friends, like George Garrity, Jim Moran, and Jim Brennan.

It was at Holy Cross that serious pursuit of women commenced for me. I can only tell you that I did much better with my studies than I did with women. I didn't understand them then, and I still don't.

One of the unsettling aspects of those early days at Holy Cross had to do with the Korean War. The Communist army of North

---

[1] Gordie Lockbaum (Holy Cross '88) was inducted into the National Football Foundation and College Hall of Fame in August 2001. He played offense, defense, and on all special teams! In 1986 he was fifth in the Heisman Trophy voting and third in 1987. He joined two other Holy Cross players inducted into the Hall of Fame, George Connor and Bill Osmanski, as well as two Holy Cross coaches, Frank Cavanagh and Eddie Anderson.

Korea had thrown back the government forces of the Republic of Korea so that the latter was reduced to a desperate defense of a relatively small perimeter around the seaport city of Pusan, which was on the south coast of South Korea. In 1950, President Truman committed United States forces to support the United Nations' effort to defeat Communist aggression in Korea, and the draft was accelerated dramatically. My classmates and I were, of course, eligible for the draft, but I wanted to finish college before serving in the military.

All of the services offered officer programs for college students. The program offered by the Marine Corps was known as the Platoon Leaders Class, and involved going away for two summers for training during college, being commissioned on graduation from college, attending Officers Basic School at Quantico, Virginia, for nine months, and then assuming duties in the line.

When I was a kid and misbehaved in front of my father, he would say to me, "What are you, a wiseguy or a marine?" I had no idea what he was talking about, but I knew enough to realize I had better stop doing whatever I was doing. As I got older, I realized that my father, during his days in the Navy in World War I, obviously had crossings with marines, who, among other things, served as sort of a police force for the Navy. But it was clear that he respected marines and that he would be proud if I joined the Marine Corps—and so I enrolled in the Marine Corps Platoon Leaders Class.

On April 10, 1951, in the spring of my sophomore year, President Truman electrified the country when he relieved General Douglas MacArthur as the supreme commander of the United Nations forces in Korea and replaced him with Lieutenant General Matthew B. Ridgeway.

MacArthur's tactics in Korea had been brilliant, including an amphibious landing at Inchon, led by the Marines under the command of General Lewis B. "Chesty" Puller. Victory was almost in hand, until the intervention of Red China. Truman was deeply concerned about precipitating a full-blown land war in Asia, and he emphatically ruled out any attack on Red China in retaliation.

MacArthur, on the other hand, *insisted* upon striking back against Red China. And from a purely military viewpoint, MacArthur was right. But Truman's responsibilities went far beyond that, and in my judgment his decision was correct. In response to questions put to him by Senator Brian McMahon of Connecticut during the so-called MacArthur Hearings in the spring of 1951, MacArthur admitted in substance that he had not fully assessed and was not prepared for an all-out land war in Asia. Truman's position was in keeping with his overall policy of Russian "containment," which he had commenced years before with his support of Greece.

Following his removal, MacArthur toured the nation, and on April 19, 1951, he addressed a joint session of Congress. I and most of my fellow students at Holy Cross skipped class to listen to him on the radio. During the defense of his conduct, he made the following point: "Once war is forced upon us, there is no other alternative than to apply every available means to bring it to a swift end. . . . In war, there is no substitute for victory."

But his most memorable words came at the end of his speech:

> The world has turned over many times since I took the oath on the plain at West Point, and the hopes and dreams have long since vanished, but I still remember the refrain of one of the most popular barracks ballads of that day which proclaimed most proudly that "old soldiers never die; they just fade away." And like the old soldier of that ballad, I now close my military career and just fade away, an old soldier who tried to do his duty as God gave him the light to see that duty. Good-bye.

Such is the impetuosity of youth and the incredible power of great public speaking that by the time MacArthur had finished his speech, I wanted Truman impeached! Although I know he was wrong, I remain an enormous admirer of MacArthur to this day. I urge you to read *American Caesar: Douglas MacArthur* (1979) by William Manchester.

Fascinating as all of those highest-level events were, the end result for me personally was that I spent the following summer at the Marine Corps Recruit Depot at Parris Island, South Carolina. I boarded the train at the old Pennsylvania Station in New York City, a breathtakingly magnificent structure. Those who remember it mourn its loss. In destroying it, the Pennsylvania Railroad did a great disservice to generations of travelers. As a result of that abomination, the New York City Landmarks Preservation Commission was established.

I had visited Florida with my uncle Tom as a child, but I hadn't experienced the kind of racial discrimination that then prevailed in the South. As a rising junior in college, I was appalled and horrified by what I saw at the railroad stations at which we stopped: separate rest rooms for "Colored," "Colored" entrances, "Colored" waiting rooms and "Colored" water fountains. Those signs screamed out, "Black people are inferior to white people." I thought about the pain and degradation that blacks, and particularly black children, must have felt in that environment.

I later learned that blacks in the South were matter-of-factly referred to as "niggers" and treated as objects rather than as human beings. Many Southerners who employed blacks had a highly offensive paternalistic attitude toward them. Even worse was the treatment blacks received at the hands of some poor whites who disparaged blacks simply to make themselves feel better and superior. All of this flew in the face of everything I had been taught from the time I was a boy. Thank God, most of that has changed.

At Parris Island, our drill instructors herded us off the train to the recruit depot, shaved our heads, gave us shots for everything under the sun, provided us with clothing and M1 rifles, and led us to the Quonset huts in which we would reside for the next ten weeks. Drill instructors in the Marine Corps are by definition mean, nasty sons of bitches. It's part of their job: they are expected to demean and abuse recruits so as to make them feel like nonhumans. The underlying concept has to do with instantaneous response to command in a combat setting. In that regard, the elimination of individuality is of extreme importance. And for us, there was something added to the mix: we were college students and presumably destined for commissions in the Marine Corps! I won't tell you what our drill instructors called us, except to say that it was not nice.

Reveille was at 5 A.M. We had standing inspections, endless marches, military tactics, calisthenics, and bayonet and hand-to-hand combat training. We had lessons on Marine Corps history and the rules of military courtesy. We fired the M1 rifle, the Browning automatic rifle, the carbine, the .45-caliber pistol, the .50-caliber water-cooled machine gun, the .30-caliber air-cooled machine gun, the bazooka, and mortars. We threw hand grenades. There were films galore on sanitation and the avoidance of venereal diseases. There were Quonset hut inspections. There were the penalties such as shaving with your helmet on (if you failed to shave properly) and sleeping with your rifle (if you dropped it or failed to remember your rifle number).

Our senior drill instructor was a Southerner by the name of Staff Sergeant Clicker. Every drill instructor at Parris Island adopted his own particular cadence when drilling troops. The standard cadence was "One, two, three, four; one, two, three, four," but there were hundreds of variations and voice inflections. Sergeant Clicker's cadence was unique. I listened to it carefully, practiced it, and mastered it.

During training at Parris Island, there came a time when each member of the platoon acted as the platoon commander for a day. When you assumed that role, you were in charge of marching the platoon to and from wherever the schedule of the day required, be it meals, classrooms, the parade grounds, staging areas, or anywhere else. When my day came to act as platoon commander, my cadence was Clicker's cadence! The platoon went into a state of controlled hysteria, and everybody was wondering how Clicker would react—including me! Thanks be to God, he loved it! In fact, he liked it so much that he had me march the platoon to evening chow regularly. Many platoons came together at the mess hall, and Clicker wanted to show me off—or, more accurately, show himself off. I never failed him, and we got along just fine. I still have fond memories of him.[2]

On those occasions when we were granted liberty, we went to one of three places. The closest was Beaufort, South Carolina. There was really nothing there except a couple of bars, and it wasn't much fun. (This, of course, was long before Pat Conroy put Beaufort on the map with his 1987 novel, *The Prince of Tides*.) When we had more extended liberty, we went to either Savannah, Georgia, or Charleston, South Carolina, both of which were interesting cities and very different from the cities I knew in the North.

The summer after my junior year, I was sent to Camp Goetche in Quantico, Virginia, for ten weeks of additional training. The training was not as stringent as it was at Parris Island, but it wasn't as much fun, either.

---

[2] Sergeant, I'd love to hear from you!

By that time, I had begun thinking seriously about becoming a lawyer. In my senior year, I applied to Fordham Law School in New York City. It was the only law school I applied to, and I was accepted. I wrote the Marine Corps a letter requesting a deferment so that I could attend law school before going on active duty, and I enclosed my academic records from Holy Cross. To be perfectly frank, I didn't think I had a prayer. To my amazement, I was deferred. The moral: it never hurts to give it a shot—you never know!

This, of course, meant no more summers training at Parris Island, Quantico, or anywhere else, at least until I graduated law school. I was elated!

At the rifle range at Parris Island, South Carolina, summer of 1951.

II

THE LAW AND PUBLIC SERVICE

4

Fordham Law School
and Challenge

I MOVED BACK HOME to New York City and started Fordham Law School in September of 1953. I had been living away from home for eight years—four years at Cranwell, four years at Holy Cross and two summers with the Marines. It was a new experience to commute to school by subway from my home in Stuyvesant Town. The law school was located at 302 Broadway in Lower Manhattan. (It subsequently moved uptown to the Lincoln Center complex in the 1960s, and 302 Broadway was demolished in 1962. A federal government building currently occupies the site.) The campus, to the extent that there was one, consisted of a local bar known as the Chambers. It was located on Chambers Street, below street level, and it was a very popular Fordham Law School hangout.

The Fordham School of Education had space in the same building as the law school. My wife, Jackie, attended the School of Education while I was attending the law school, and that's how we met.

Law school was hard work, but I found it fascinating. We used the casebook method, whereby we read significant legal cases and attempted to distinguish or reconcile the legal principles that emerged. In examinations, we were called upon to apply those principles to new fact patterns. It was wonderfully stimulating intellectually, very much like mathematics but far more interesting. The law deals not with sterile mathematical principles but rather with human principles, and their application is infinitely more meaningful.

At the end of the first year, I was invited to become a member of the *Fordham Law Review,* and in my third and final year I served as its articles editor. I found the *Law Review* work to be an education within an education, and well worth the enormous time demands that adversely effect grades.

During my first year in law school (1953/54), the nation was mesmerized by the televised Army–McCarthy hearings. There were seventy-two Senate committee sessions, thirty-five witnesses, forty-two exhibits, and 2,972 pages of testimony. Senator Joseph R. McCarthy of Wisconsin was the chairman of the Senate Committee on Government Operations, which conducted the hearings.

The nation's opinion was sharply divided with respect to McCarthy, who was doggedly pursuing Communist sympathizers in the U.S. Feelings ran deep, and heated arguments broke out regularly in the media and across America. Initially I favored McCarthy. There was no question that philosophically Communism was international in reach and that the surreptitious infiltration into other governments, especially ours, was an extremely important factor in the spread of Communist doctrine. Klaus Fuchs and the Rosenbergs had recently been convicted of passing atomic secrets to the Soviets, and Alger Hiss had been convicted of perjury in connection with spying on behalf of the Soviet Union. And there were others.

But in the end, McCarthy's outrageous and continuing excesses brought him down. The final blow was delivered by a crafty, cagey old codger by the name of Joe Welsh, a partner in the Boston firm of Hale and Dore, which was representing the U.S. Army. Welsh had on his staff a young lawyer by the name of Frederick Fisher, who was a member of the National Lawyers Guild, which had been listed as subversive by the House Un-American Activities Committee (HUAC). Fisher had been involved in the organization of the Guild's Boston chapter, but there was no evidence that he was a Communist. In fact, he had resigned from the Guild in 1950 after learning of a connection between the Boston chapter and the local communist organization.

McCarthy was aware of Fisher's background, and as a result he and Welsh worked out an agreement whereby McCarthy would not raise the subject publicly and Welsh promised not to allude to alleged efforts by one of McCarthy's counsels, a young lawyer named Roy Cohn, to avoid the draft. But during a heated exchange in the public proceedings, McCarthy violated the agreement and attacked young Fisher. At first, Welsh implored McCarthy to stop—but he wouldn't.

Finally, Welsh turned to McCarthy and said, "Let us not assassinate this lad further, Senator. You have done enough. Have you no sense of decency, sir, at long last? Have you left no sense of decency?" McCarthy was finished, and I learned a vital lesson on just how effective good advocacy can be!

Throughout my days in law school, the subject of the Fifth Amendment was of keen interest to the bench and bar because of the Army–McCarthy hearings and other events. We published an article on the Fifth Amendment in the *Fordham Law Review*, by C. Dickerman Williams, that attracted national notoriety. The demand for copies was so overwhelming that we had to do a special printing of that single article, and it was cited and quoted extensively.

In 1955, during my second year in law school, my beloved Dodgers beat the loathed and despised New York Yankees in the World Series! Gil Hodges, Jackie Robinson, Pee Wee Reese, Billy Cox, Roy Campanella, Carl Furillo, Duke Snider, Andy Pafko, Johnny Podres, Joe Black, Carl Erskine, Clem Labine, Preacher Roe—the "Boys of Summer" were the world's champions![1] Brooklyn was in a state of pandemonium. For years, Brooklyn Dodgers fans had been saying, "Wait until next year." One headline proudly proclaimed: "*This* is Next Year!" For years, the Dodgers had been known as the Brooklyn Bums and had been portrayed by a magnificent cartoonist, Leo O'Mealia, on the sports pages as a bum. My favorite front page appeared in the *Daily News* the day after the final game of the World Series, in which the Dodgers beat the Yankees. There was the traditional caricature of the Brooklyn Dodgers bum saying: "Who's a Bum?"

The taste of victory is sweetest when you've been loyal to a team throughout its trials, tribulations, disappointments, and darkest hours. Interestingly, I received telephone calls and notes of congratulations from friends from all over, including Waterbu-

---

[1] Read *The Boys of Summer* (1987), by Roger Kahn.

rians and Bostonians, and I was very gracious in victory. It's easy, and it makes you feel even better!

At 8:15 P.M. on April 8, 1956, as I was approaching graduation from law school, Staff Sergeant Matthew McKeon, a junior drill instructor at Parris Island, was marching his platoon of seventy-five recruits into Ribbon Creek in an effort to instill "esprit" into his flagging and low-scoring charges. A number of them veered into deep waters in the darkness, and six of them became mired in thick mud, panicked, and drowned. While an unusually strong current was also a factor, five of the six were nonswimmers. McKeon tried desperately to save one of them and was the last one out of the water. In addition, he was a decorated Korean War veteran with a previously unblemished record. He assumed full responsibility for the tragedy and never deviated in that regard. He was charged with a general court-martial and was represented pro bono by Emile Zola Berman. The case received national attention. It wasn't just McKeon who was on trial, it was the entire Marine Corps—and its training methods in particular. Moreover, the case came at a time when the Marine Corps had budgeting problems and was redefining its mission in light of the development of atomic weaponry.

The McKeon case was of particular interest to me because of my earlier experience at Parris Island and the fascinating legal issues involved. McKeon was later convicted and sentenced to loss of rank to private, a dishonorable discharge, and nine months of hard labor (later reduced to three months). In 1998, during an interview with Arnold Abrams of *Newsday,* a still tormented and tortured seventy-three-year-old Matthew McKeon sobbed: "I wish I went down with them."

I graduated from Fordham Law School in May of 1956 and was commissioned as a second lieutenant in the Marine Corps. Graduation was at the Fordham University campus at Rose Hill in the Bronx, and my father was present. I was in uniform, and after the graduation ceremony he saluted me. I thought to myself, "What a joke—this great American patriot saluting *me*." I returned his salute, shook his hand, and embraced him. I had the overwhelming joy of knowing I had made him *enormously* proud.

While Fordham Law School at 302 Broadway didn't have much of a campus, it had a host of extraordinary professors—Ignatius Wilkenson, I. Maurice Wormser, George Bacon, Leonard Manning, John Calamari, Joseph Crowley, Ray O'Keefe, Gene Keefe, Pete Thomas, and a young professor by the name of William Hughes Mulligan, who was later to become the dean of the law school, a judge of the Second Circuit Court of Appeals, and the best after-dinner speaker I've ever heard! He was a spectacular teacher, and I took every course he taught, including Insurance Law, undoubtedly the most boring course in the curriculum—but not with Mulligan! Those professors made Fordham Law School a delightful and exhilarating intellectual challenge, and they instilled in us a keen sense of morality and decency.

Because I was going into the service, I could have avoided taking the New York State bar exam and been admitted to practice law in New York on waiver. I didn't feel comfortable with being admitted on waiver and, accordingly, took the bar exam just before going on active duty.

In 1988, I received the Medal of Achievement from Fordham Law School at its annual luncheon held at the Waldorf-Astoria. My dear friend John D. Feerick, the dean of the law school, introduced me. He said that he had reviewed my law school file and found a letter my father had written to the school when I applied for admission in 1953. It said, "This is the $50 money-order deposit you wanted for my son James. What do I get for the $50?" The hall exploded with laughter, and so did I. I hadn't known about it until that moment. Here are a few words from my address to the audience that day:

> When I began Fordham Law School in September of 1953, more than thirty-five years ago, it was located at 302 Broadway and was substantially different in many ways from what it is today. . . . At that time, there were two criteria for admission to the law school: firstly, you had to be free and clear of all communicable diseases—and secondly, you would not be admitted if, at the time of your application, you were under indictment for the commission of a major felony. These criteria, however, were not rigidly enforced. As a matter of fact, in a limited number of cases, *both* criteria were completely waived! You may be interested to know that my old friend—Professor Constantine N. Katsoris—was admitted to the law school pursuant to such a double waiver. . . .

302 Broadway was frankly somewhat of a disappointment. In order to get to the classrooms, you had to go through a Chock Full o' Nuts coffee shop. The law school had procured an easement from Chock Full o' Nuts, under the terms of which each Fordham Law School student was required to buy a minimum of two cups of coffee and four doughnuts—whenever entering or leaving the building. While tuition in 1953 was only nine hundred dollars per year, the added cost of coffee and doughnuts placed the Law School among the most expensive in the country. . . .

I am proud of my law school because it is carrying out a sacred mission. Our law school has been and under John Feerick continues to graduate brilliant young lawyers, who are imbued with a sense of decency and morality. They are not simply interested in making money but want to make a contribution to the common good, improve the lot of other human beings, and make their lives count.

My son Dennis was in the audience, together with all of the members of my family (including my aunt Anne Shanahan), and I could hear his raucous laughter at every joke throughout the speech. He maintains to this day that it was my best speech ever. He may be right—but then again, *it's so hard to judge!*

5

The Marines and
the Good Times

ON AUGUST 1, 1956, a week after I took the bar exam, I reported to Officers Basic School at Camp Upshur in Quantico, Virginia, and began nine months of officers' infantry training. Although we were all second lieutenants at Basic School, in reality we were little more than what we had been at Parris Island and Quantico during summer tours. The platoon commanders were captains, and the company commanders were majors. We lived in Quonset huts and did many of the same kinds of things we had done during our summer tours, although there was more of it and additional things to learn. We were introduced to training in amphibious landings, tanks, and the relatively new offensive concept of "vertical envelopment," which brought helicopters into play on the offense. We received training in night fighting and engaged in simulated three-day wars against "school troops" who utilized the same tactics that the North Koreans had utilized in the Korean War.

About two months after arriving at Camp Upshur, I received word that my father had died. I took emergency leave, had a black armband sewn in the left sleeve of my uniform, and went back to Waterbury to attend the wake at Mulville's and the funeral Mass at St. Margaret's Church—the same rituals I had experienced when my grandfather died. I remained in uniform throughout because I knew my father would have wanted it that way. On the day of the funeral Mass, I rode in the first car behind the hearse, with Aunt Nell, Uncle Tom, and Uncle Den. The entourage came to a halt in front of St. Margaret's, and everyone got out of their cars and waited for the pallbearers to carry the flag-draped coffin up the church steps. When they did so, I saluted.

About a month later, I was informed that I had passed the bar exam. While I regret that my father didn't live to hear that news, I derived great comfort in the knowledge that it was infinitely more important to him that I had become a Marine Corps officer.

After I graduated from Basic School, I was assigned to the staff legal office at Marine Corps Schools, Quantico, Virginia. I simply moved from Camp Upshur in the "boondocks" (the woods) to "Mainside" (civilization). Marine Corps Schools had general courts-martial jurisdiction, and accordingly I would be prosecuting and defending the most serious offenses under the United States Code of Military Justice. My boss was Navy Lieutenant Commander Joseph B. McDivitt, the staff judge advocate, who reported directly to General Merrill B. Twinning, the commanding officer of Marine Corps Schools.

By the time I arrived at Mainside, my hair was prematurely and *substantially* gray. As a result, I looked considerably older than my peers. Despite my apparent advanced age (I'm sure that most figured me for at least forty), I was only a second lieutenant and wore *no* medals (because I hadn't earned any).

From time to time, the officers in the staff legal office would be called upon to drill troops awaiting separation from the Marine Corps, and I pulled that duty regularly because I was so junior in rank. I had a strong command voice, and as a result of my training under Sergeant Clicker, I knew how to drill troops in an impressive way. (Of course, I used Clicker's cadence.) As a result, most of the troops that I drilled concluded that I was "mustang"—that is to say, I had come through the ranks! Many also concluded that the reason I didn't wear my medals was that I had so many! I would get questions like "Mr. Gill, didn't I see you at Tarawa?" or "Didn't our paths cross at Okinawa?" My answer was always the same: "I'd rather not get into that, son." On a few such occasions, I was sorely tempted to feign a slight limp—but I restrained myself.

One day, Commander McDivitt called me into his office and told me that General Twinning had some serious income tax and domestic-relations problems that he wanted to discuss. He told me he was assigning me to the case because I was the member of the legal staff most recently out of law school and therefore most conversant with those subjects. At least that's what he said. Fortunately, I handled the general's problems in a manner that was much to his satisfaction. I also assisted his house aides (domestic help) when they got into difficulty in Washington, D.C., on a number of occasions. Thereafter I could do no wrong.

Later I assumed the additional duties of giving general legal advice to the troops at Marine Corps Schools and protecting their overall interests. At that time, there were a number of car dealers between Quantico, Virginia, and Washington, D.C., who were taking advantage of our young marines. They would extract a substantial deposit, and as soon as a payment was missed, they would repossess the car and resell it. Those car dealers knew that failure to pay a just debt was a court-martial offense, and they took full advantage of it. In addition, some unscrupulous salesmen were selling freezers and meal plans to our married marines. They invariably promised them steaks, chops, and turkeys and then provided them with scrawny chickens, inferior hamburger meat, and dried-up frankfurters.

I published a blacklist of all the car dealers and meal-plan providers I concluded had been dealing unfairly with our marines. When my blacklist came to the attention of the Chamber of Commerce in Washington, D.C., it requested a meeting with General Twinning. Twinning invited me to attend. The Chamber of Commerce representative listed his grievances, and Twinning asked me to respond; I cited one case of abuse after another, in detail. Twinning threw the Chamber of Commerce representative out on his ear, shook my hand, and said, "Well done." I felt great! The blacklists remained and indeed were supplemented.

In retrospect, my days on the Staff Legal Office at Marine Corps Schools were among the best days of my life. I had money in my pocket for the first time, and I was living in the BOQ (Bachelor Officers' Quarters), which was enormous fun. I was doing work that I loved, and I made friendships that have endured to this day. Moreover, the ratio of women to men in nearby Washington was eight to one. I briefly considered making the Marine Corps a career but concluded reluctantly that in the long run it would not be desirable from a family viewpoint.

I considered taking a year off and traveling around the world but finally decided against it. *That* was a mistake. It was the last opportunity that I had to do such a thing, and I've have been working ever since. James and Gillian: if you ever have such an opportunity, grab it!

I had the high honor of having breakfast with General Bernard Krulak, the commandant of the Marine Corps, in the Board of Governors room of the New York Stock Exchange on November 11, 1998. I took the occasion to have a little fun with him. His father had also been a general officer in the Marine Corps and indeed almost became commandant himself.

During the breakfast I said to the commandant: "General, I served as the trial counsel (prosecutor) for general courts-martial at Quantico while your father was stationed there during 1957 and 1958, and I can report to you that at no time during that entire time frame was your father ever charged with a general courts-martial!" He roared and went on to tell me how delighted he was to receive my report.

General Krulak and I on the floor of the New York Stock Exchange on November 11, 1999.

Vincent Sardi, owner of the famous New York restaurant, is a marine. (There are no ex-marines, former marines, or retired marines—once a marine, always a marine.) Every year at Christmastime, he graciously hosts a party to raise money for Toys for Tots, a great Marine Corps tradition spanning many decades. Marines, be they on active duty, reservists, or retirees, are invited. Traditionally there are two speakers, a marine on active duty and an inactive marine.

In 1998, I was chosen as the inactive Marine Corps speaker, and I used the opportunity to share some memories of Sergeant Clicker:

> My drill instructor at Parris Island was Staff Sergeant Clicker. My first individual contact with him was when we were in formation and he was walking the line. He stopped in front of me and said, "Where are you from?"
>
> "Waterbury, Connecticut, sir," I answered, whereupon Clicker barked, "Goddammit, I knew it—I knew it the first time I laid eyes on your miserable ass." In the meantime I was saying to myself, *How did he know? How could he tell? What is there about me that told him that I'm from Waterbury? There are millions of cities in this country, and he picked out my hometown—it's a miracle—he must know everything.*
>
> My second confrontation also took place while we were in formation. Clicker came down the line, stopped in front of me, and asked: "Do you like me?" He had put the same question to another member of the platoon earlier, and the answer came back, "No, sir." Clicker then demanded to know each and every reason why he *didn't* like Clicker. It was excruciating. I wasn't going to fall into that trap, and so I answered, "Yes, sir." It was the worst mistake of my life. For five full minutes, he called me everything under the sun—including a transvestite, despite the fact that I didn't own a stitch of women's clothing.
>
> My third encounter with Clicker came when I banged on the door of his Quonset hut and called out my name as per instructions. My purpose was to get permission to leave the platoon area in order to go to the head [the toilet].
>
> A booming voice bellowed from within, "I can't hear you." After five more knocks and listening to "I can't hear you" five more times, I was admitted to the sanctum sanctorum. He asked, "What do you want?"
>
> "Permission to go to the head, sir," I responded.
>
> Clicker looked at me disdainfully and asked, "Will you piss in your pants if I don't let you go?"
>
> *This is a trick question,* I said to myself—and my mind began to race.
>
> *If I tell him No, he won't let me go.*

If I tell him Yes and then I don't, he'll accuse me of lying, and that will be the end of me.

So I answered, "Eventually, sir."

Whereupon Clicker leapt from his chair red-faced and screamed out at the top of his lungs: "When I ask you a question, I only want to hear one of three answers: 'Yes, sir,' 'No, sir,' or 'I don't know, sir.'"

I then gave serious consideration to answering: "I don't know, sir." But then I thought, *How can I possibly tell him that I don't know whether I'm going to piss in my pants?* So I answered, "Yes, sir." To which he responded, "Well, piss in them. Get out."

There is no need to get into what followed.

6

Hogan's Office

MY FIRST JOB after the Marine Corps was as an assistant district attorney of New York County under the late, great Frank S. Hogan. Hogan had earned a national reputation as an able, fearless, and incorruptible prosecutor, and he hailed from Waterbury. Hogan had inherited the office from Tom Dewey, the legendary racket-buster and former governor of New York who ran unsuccessfully for President on the Republican ticket against Harry Truman in 1948. (Truman, in my judgment, will be ranked among the greatest Presidents in the history of our country. His defeat of Dewey in 1948 was hands-down the most spectacular upset in the history of American politics. He had *everything* going against him—and he prevailed. I think he won by persistence and force of personality. For more on the subject, read David McCullough's *Truman* [1992], which is one of the best biographies I've ever read.)

Hogan was a unique DA in that his office was nonpartisan and apolitical. No politician, or anyone else for that matter, could reach into his office and influence a case. He hired almost exclusively from law schools, and *no one,* especially political leaders, had any say whatsoever as to whom he hired. Assistant DAs were required to work full-time and were not permitted to engage in any other legal pursuits. Hogan precluded us from going to nightclubs or racetracks, on the premise that he did not want us seen with the unsavory characters who frequented such places. Courtesy toward the public-at-large, and everyone with whom we dealt professionally, was a matter of utmost importance. All correspondence had to be answered within three days.

Hogan's office was dynamic. He didn't wait for the police to bring cases into his office but rather went on the offensive in areas he deemed important, such as organized crime, labor racketeering, and public corruption. He had a squad of Police Department detectives attached to his office, and he also hired private investigators to work solely for him. He used those investigators in the most sensitive investigations. His conviction record was extraordinary, and those of us who worked for him couldn't wait to get to work in the morning. We were involved in important business—the protection of the lives and property of New Yorkers. We knew that we could go after *anyone* in New York County who violated the penal code and that he would stand behind us! We all pulled together and helped each other.

Hogan's office was departmentalized. New hires started in the Complaint Bureau, where you would listen to complaints from citizens who came in off the street. Joe Stone was in charge of the Complaint Bureau, and he had an utter fixation about prosecuting persons who committed the crime of false and misleading advertising. Indeed, it was somewhat bizarre. Because of his all-consuming absorption with the subject, he would appoint an assistant DA to administer all other responsibilities of the bureau. Shortly after I joined the office, he asked me to do that job. I was delighted to oblige and it was great fun.

One day, a woman by the name of Frances Friedman came into the Complaint Bureau and was interviewed by my friend and colleague Allen Schwartz. She had been experiencing serious physical and emotional problems, and in her desperation she had turned to a gypsy by the name of Volga Adams for relief. Volga was the wife of Blackie Adams, the so-called King of the Gypsies, who was the subject of Peter Maas's 1975 book of the same title.

After a lot of preliminary mumbo jumbo, Volga advised poor Frances that the source of all her troubles was her money and that the answer to all of her problems was its destruction. There followed an absurd ritual whereby $118,000 that Frances turned over to the gypsy was allegedly burned in a garbage can. During the ritual, Volga held a chicken over the fire and, according to Volga, the bird was killed by inhaling the smoke from the evil money. An examination of the chicken's neck might have revealed a different cause of death!

Allen reported the case to me, and we indicted Volga immediately, only to learn that she had fled the jurisdiction. A fugitive warrant was issued for her arrest, and eventually she was arrested in Alabama. The governor of Alabama issued a rendition warrant ordering her to be returned to New York to answer the larceny charge. Volga fought her return through the Alabama courts, unsuccessfully. Just before her case was to be heard by Alabama's highest court, Volga switched lawyers and hired Alabama's highway commissioner, whereupon the governor withdrew his rendition warrant! As a result, Volga had asylum in Alabama. Hogan was furious and I was madder than Hogan.

Volga later left Alabama and was arrested in Miami on the still-outstanding fugitive warrant. The judge in Miami granted her bail, instead of holding her in custody as he *clearly should have* since she was a *fugitive*. We, of course, realized immediately that we did not have a friendly forum in Miami.

The governor of New York asked the governor of Florida to issue a rendition warrant and a hearing was scheduled to be held in Tallahassee, Florida's capital, as to whether the governor of Florida should do so. When Volga elected to attend, Hogan sent me to Tallahassee to attend the hearing. Under normal circumstances such a hearing is pro forma; no evidence is taken, and the governor issues the rendition warrant automatically *several days later*. Because of the special circumstances of this case, we prevailed upon the governor to issue the rendition warrant *immediately* and to have Volga arrested *before she could leave Tallahassee*. That's what happened, and as a result Volga had her court hearing in Tallahassee instead of Miami where we certainly would have lost! The Tallahassee court ordered that she be returned to New York immediately. Now it was her turn to be angry!

Hogan and I were elated. He assigned Burt Roberts, the most senior trial assistant in the office to try the case. Halfway through the trial, Volga turned to Roberts, a longstanding bachelor, and with fire in her eyes said, "I give you the gypsy curse: you will *never* marry and you will *never* have children." Roberts responded, "I give you a worse curse, the Jewish curse: you will roam the face of the earth for the rest of your days and never find a home." The media had a field day. The jury was hung, and Volga wound up pleading to a lesser charge. Roberts overcame the gypsy's curse late in life, when he married his delightful bride, Gerheld. And the gypsy overcame Roberts's curse by finding a home in jail!

The next step in the office progression following the Complaint Bureau was the Indictment Bureau, where we presented case after case to the grand jury. In the main, they were cases brought to the office by the New York Police Department. Hogan always stressed that it was the job of the district attorney's office not only to prosecute the guilty *but to protect the innocent.* Accordingly, the standard he set with respect to indicting a person was higher than the standard required by law. Not only did he require evidence with respect to all elements of the crime but required a likelihood that the defendant would be convicted by a petit jury.

From the Indictment Bureau, I moved on to the Special Sessions Bureau, which tried misdemeanors (crimes for which the penalty was one year in prison or less). There were two assistants in each part and each of us tried four or five cases a day. As a result, we learned a lot about New York City and the people who lived in it. After a while, in my travels about New York, I saw things happening that others were totally unaware of—hookers, pimps, chicken hawks, bookmakers, numbers runners, pickpockets, drug pushers, you name it.

Next in the progression was the Supreme Court Bureau, which tried felony jury cases. We tried every kind of felony except homicides, which were handled by the Homicide Bureau. In the Supreme Court Bureau, it was common for defendants to plead guilty during the course of the trial. In fact, very few cases went to verdict. Of the hundreds of cases I prepared and started, only thirteen felony trials went to verdict, and of those, twelve were convictions and one was a hung jury. The case that ended with a hung jury was an armed robbery, one-witness identification case. One of the jurors was an Orthodox Jew who refused to find the defendant guilty because Talmudic law required *two* witnesses for a guilty finding! We didn't see that one coming. (The defendant later pleaded guilty.)

I had another one-witness identification case that involved a young black man who was charged with robbing an Italian delicatessen at gunpoint in Little Italy. The police interviewed the delicatessen's owner, named Margiata, immediately after the robbery. During the interview, Mr. Margiata said that the person who had robbed him was about thirty-five years old. The defendant was only twenty-two, and his attorney made a great to-do about Margiata's original statement—and understandably so.

As I mentioned earlier, my hair was prematurely *very* gray. In my re-direct examination of Mr. Margiata, I asked him to guess my age. Mr. Margiata's answer was, "Oh, I know-a you, Mr. Gill—you prematurely gray—you a young man."

I said: "Yes, Mr. Margiata, but how old would you say I am?"

"Oh," he said, "you much, much younger than you look, you prematurely gray, but you got a baby face."

"But Mr. Margiata, tell me, how old do you think I am?"

Whereupon he responded, "I'm, a think-a you maybe about—forty-five." I was not yet thirty, and when he gave his response, the courtroom exploded with laughter (I'm pleased to report). Shortly thereafter, the jury found the defendant guilty. Who says prematurely gray hair is a bad thing? It served me well until about twenty years ago, when my age caught up with my hair!

On television and in the movies when courtroom trials are portrayed, there is frequently a very dramatic moment when an unforeseen piece of evidence drops from the heavens and is decisive: a "deus ex machina." That almost never happens in the real world. Both sides prepare their cases thoroughly, and there are rarely surprises. However, I had a deus ex machina in one of the cases that I tried when I was in Hogan's office.

The defendant was a major drug seller in Spanish Harlem. In those days, undercover narcotics officers posing as addicts or small-scale peddlers would make purchases from drug sellers. They would make three or four such purchases from the same seller to solidify the case, but the seller would not be arrested until days after the final purchase. The purpose of delaying the arrest was to protect the identity of the undercover officer so that he would be able to continue his undercover work in the area in which he was functioning. We had a very stringent rule in the office at that time: if a defendant charged with selling narcotics to an undercover narcotics officer went to trial and thereby exposed that officer, we would ask the judge to impose the maximum sentence if a conviction resulted. Such cases always ended in convictions, and the judges would invariably impose the maximum sentence. Selling any kind of narcotics in any amount was regarded as very serious in those days—and the narcotics cops, unlike some of their brothers in the areas of gambling and prostitution, were on the level. Everyone connected with the criminal justice system was aware of the above-described situation, and very few defendants in those kinds of cases ever went to trial. They would plea-bargain. But the defendant in my case was relatively young, had no prior record, and decided to take a chance. His defense was that he was a decent citizen; that he had never peddled drugs and that the police had arrested the wrong man—that it was, in short, a case of mistaken identity.

My undercover officer identified the defendant as the person from whom he had purchased narcotics on a number of occasions, and his "backup" corroborated his testimony. He further testified that the defendant was Spanish and called himself "El Aguilar," which is Spanish for "The Eagle."

The defendant took the stand, protested his innocence at great length, and stated that he would produce several witnesses to show he was elsewhere at the time of the alleged sales. At some point during his direct testimony, I noticed that he seemed to be concealing his hands. When I cross-examined him, I got as close as I could to observe his hands. Eventually it became apparent that he had letters on the knuckles of both of his hands—but I couldn't make them out. Finally I said to him, "Let me see your hands." He refused and his lawyer objected. The objection was overruled. The letters on the knuckles of his hands spelled "El Aguilar"!

Among the most highly respected assistants that served in Hogan's office during my time was Mel Glass, who later became the chief of the Complaint Bureau and a Criminal Court judge. Many would say he was the best. We came into the office at the same time, and we became and remain close friends.

Mel's involvement in the Wylie-Hoffert double-murder case provided Hogan's office with one of its most shining hours.

On August 28, 1963, Emily Hoffert and Janice Wylie were brutally murdered in the apartment they shared at 57 East Eighty-eighth Street in Manhattan, which is in the Twenty-third Precinct. Emily and Janice were very attractive young career women who were well on their way to the top in their respective fields. Emily was the daughter of a Chicago doctor, and Janice's uncle was the noted author Philip Wylie.

The particulars of the killings were gruesome. Both died of vicious multiple stab wounds, and Emily's head was almost severed from her body. The murder scene was drenched with blood, and when I saw the photographs from the murder scene, I almost threw up.

Physical evidence suggested that the killer had hit both women on the head with a Coke bottle and that while Janice was rendered unconscious, Emily had fought for her life, like a tigress—thus the severity of the damage to her neck.

The killer placed the bodies side by side next to a bed and covered them with a blue blanket. He then took a shower, meticulously cleaned the knives that he had used in the killings, placed them on a radiator, and left.

The case received national attention, and the police were under enormous pressure to apprehend the killer. A young black man by the name of George Whitmore confessed to the Wylie-Hoffert murders and two other murders in Brooklyn, where he lived. Whitmore's final confession was taken by Peter Koste, an assistant in the homicide bureau. Whitmore's confession was replete with minute details about the killings and the interior of the apartment, and everyone concluded that Whitmore had to be the killer.

There was only one person who wasn't convinced: Mel Glass. Mel was in the Supreme Court Bureau, my bureau, and protocol barred us from interfering with a case handled by another bureau.

Nonetheless, Mel got involved—big time! He had been kept abreast of the details by a New York Police Department detective by the name of John Justy, who worked in Hogan's office. Justy had been assigned to the case as a liaison between the police and the victims' families, and accordingly was privy to the details. Justy was a superb detective—smart, honest, savvy, and very engaging. Pete Koste, who took Whitmore's final confession, shared information with Mel as well.

Mel was particularly interested in the fastidious behavior of the killer, and he discussed this aspect of the case with his sister Blanche, who was a psychiatrist. She told Mel that the killer was a person obsessed with cleanliness—he and everything around him had to be "squeaky clean." When Glass inquired as to the state of Whitmore's cleanliness at the time of his arrest, Glass was told that the suspect had been dirty and disheveled. Mel also wondered what a black kid from Brooklyn was doing in an apartment on the Upper East Side; predators like the one involved in the Wylie-Hoffert case are known to operate almost invariably in areas with which they are familiar. Al Herman, a veteran chief of the Homicide Bureau, raised the same concern.

About a year later, in October 1964, Mel learned that one Jimmy Delany had been arrested for murder by a Twenty-third Precinct detective, Pat Lappin. Delany had admitted to killing a man named Cruz but insisted that it was in self-defense. Delany claimed that Cruz had sold him a hundred-dollar bag of narcotics that turned out to be sugar; that he had confronted Cruz; and that in an ensuing fight, Cruz had attacked him with a chair leg, whereupon Delany stabbed Cruz. Other independent witnesses corroborated Delany's version of the killing. Delany also told Lappin that the police had arrested the wrong man in the Wylie-Hoffert case, and that he knew who the killer was—but he wanted a deal!

Glass asked that Delany be sent from the Tombs (the detention center for those awaiting trial in Manhattan) to the district attorney's office for questioning. Delany agreed, but also demanded immunity as to the Wylie-Hoffert case. He was assured that his requests would be met.

According to Delany, he and his wife, Marjorie, lived on the Upper East Side and had a friend and neighbor by the name of Richard Robles for whom Delany procured narcotics regularly. On one occasion while Delany was out procuring narcotics, Robles told Marjorie that he had murdered Emily Hoffert and Janice Wylie. Robles repeated his admission when Delany returned with the narcotics.

The details of Robles's statements to the Delanys were consistent with the known facts of the case, and Robles was brought in for questioning. Robles denied everything and was released! Independent corroboration was essential, since the Delanys had criminal records, and their desire to keep Delany out of jail was seen as a motive to lie. More importantly, the Whitmore confession was still in place. Glass was devastated.

But then Robles made a mistake. He continued to associate with the Delanys at their apartment, despite the fact that he knew they had given him up! Pursuant to a court order, a microphone was placed in the Delany apartment, and admissions by Robles were recorded. Glass listened to the tapes and concluded that the quality of the recordings was not sufficient for court use. Phil Robinson, an investigator on Hogan's staff, then suggested to Mel that a crystal microphone replace the carbon one that was in place. The crystal microphone had far better quality but required that a listening post be set up in close proximity. As luck would have it, the apartment next door to the Delanys' was occupied by the mother of a police officer, and she agreed to turn over her apartment. A crystal microphone was installed.

Robles made numerous incriminating admissions. At one point, he even told the Delanys that he would take a lie-detector test if he could just plant it in his mind that he hadn't killed Wylie and Hoffert! He was arrested and made a full confession in which he admitted that he had entered the apartment through the kitchen window in order to commit a burglary; that he was confronted by Janice Wylie; that he forced her to commit oral sodomy; and that Emily Hoffert entered the apartment while he was there. He went on to describe the killings and everything that happened thereafter. At one point, he said: "I go to do a bullshit burglary and I wind up killing two dames."

Robles went to trial. John F. Keenan, the office's premier trial lawyer, tried the case, and Mel assisted. Robles was convicted and sent to jail. Whitmore was exonerated. The Wylie-Hoffert case later gave rise to the television series called *Kojak,* starring Telly Savalas. By the way, Robles *was* a cleanliness fanatic, as Blanche had suggested. In my opinion, Mel Glass was *the best* I saw during my tenure in Hogan's office—and that's saying a whole hell of a lot!

In 1973, Mel left the office to go on the Criminal Court bench. I was the principal speaker at his retirement dinner, which was held at the Fifth Avenue Hotel. Excerpts from my speech can be found in appendix A.

But far more important things happened during my days in Hogan's office than any of the cases in which we were involved.

On February 7, 1959, I married my wife, Jackie, in St. Michael's Church in Jersey City, New Jersey. Marrying Jackie was the best decision I've ever made. We have three children: Patrick, born on February 23, 1960; Rose, born on September 15, 1961; and Dennis, born on October 20, 1963. They were all born at St. Vincent's Hospital in Greenwich Village. Each birth was a glorious event, and each child a joy! We had an apartment in Stuyvesant Town, and it was a great place to live and raise a family.

Now, James and Gillian, I want to tell you a bit about your mother. Rose was so beautiful that we had a portrait of her painted by Deloros Del Casio, one of the finest portrait painters in the country. The portrait took more than a year to complete and cost half of my annual salary. But it was worth every cent! Del Casio did a fabulous job. That portrait hangs in the living room of our home, in Rockville Centre, New York.

Rose was an excellent student and was extremely well behaved. She adored her older brother, Patrick, and followed him around wherever he went. Our only concern about Rose was that she was exceptionally quiet (which you may find hard to believe). I recently asked her why she had been so quiet as a child. Her answer: "I was observing."

We are all proud of Rose's accomplishments. She served as the senior deputy chief of the criminal division of the U.S. attorney's office for the Southern District of New York under Mary Jo White, and is an adjunct professor at Fordham Law School. In January 2002, Mayor Michael Bloomberg named her Commissioner of Investigation of the City of New York.

Your uncle Patrick is exceptionally bright, extremely well read, informed, sensitive, and understanding. And your uncle Dennis is principled and deeply religious, with a delightful personality and a delicious sense of humor. He is also an American history aficionado and a superb stock trader!

When I began working for Frank Hogan, I was single. Five years later, I was married with three children. My starting salary was four thousand dollars a year. While Hogan gave me a five-hundred-dollar increase every six months throughout the time I worked for him (and for which I was deeply grateful), it just wasn't enough to support my family. I had to move on.

When I told my uncle Tom that I had decided to leave Hogan's office, he urged me to get involved in the Kennedy administration. He had supported President Kennedy and had raised money for Ted Kennedy, my fellow Cranwellian who made a successful

My wife, Jackie, and our three children. Back row: Patrick, Jackie, and Den. Front: Rose.

bid for the U.S. Senate from Massachusetts shortly after his brother John became President. Although I was primarily concerned with supporting my family, I agreed to explore the prospects of becoming involved in the Kennedy administration, and my uncle Tom set up a meeting for me with Senator Kennedy in Washington.

Shortly thereafter, in February 1963, my uncle was involved in a terrible automobile accident on the West Side Highway when his driver drove into an abutment. He was taken to Downtown Hospital, where he fought valiantly to survive. He was still fighting for his life when I left for my meeting with Senator Kennedy. When I arrived, I was ushered into his office immediately. After we shook hands, he said: "Have you heard about your uncle?"

I said, "No."

"Well," he said, "I am very sorry to tell you that he died this morning." I fell to pieces.

Kennedy could not have been more gracious. He left his office so that I could be alone. After I collected myself, he had his driver take me to the airport for the return to New York. Shortly thereafter, he called to suggest another meeting. I never went back. I may disagree with Senator Kennedy on a lot of things, but I will always remember his extraordinary kindness to me on that occasion. He is a sensitive and caring man—and there's a lot to be said for that!

My uncle Tom was waked at Campbell's Funeral Parlor, on Manhattan's Upper East Side, on March 8–10, 1963. The world turned out. Francis Cardinal Spellman, Governor Nelson Rockefeller, Mayor Wagner (with whom Uncle Tom had been feuding), senators, congresspersons, business leaders, a host of people he had helped, and some who never met him but knew what he was all about.

His funeral Mass was held at St. Patrick's Cathedral on March 11, and the church was packed. The principal celebrant was my cousin Father Pat Shanahan. At the end of the Mass as the casket containing his body went past the pew in which I was seated, I thought: *Your champion is gone—and you're on your own.*

In 1973, years after I had left Hogan's office, William Vanden Heuvel ran against Hogan for the office of district attorney of

New York County, in a Democratic primary race. It was the first time in decades that Hogan had had opposition. Vanden Heuvel was the darling of the Kennedy clan, who supported him with substantial campaign contributions.

I became involved in that campaign on behalf of Hogan in a very meaningful way. I galvanized former Hogan assistants, served on the speakers' committee, raised money, and urged everyone I knew in Manhattan to vote for Hogan.

At the campaign headquarters on the night of the primary, Hogan was seated behind a desk, and the rest of us were gathered around him, when Vanden Heuvel called to concede the election. Hogan had captured some 80 percent of the vote. As always, he was very gracious during his telephone conversation with Vanden Heuvel. He congratulated him on a fine campaign and urged him to remain in public service.

When Hogan hung up the phone, I stood up, extended my hand, and said: "Congratulations, Fra—Mr. Hogan!" Even then,

Frank Hogan and the members of the Supreme Court Bureau during the Hogan years. From left to right: Maury Nadjari, Mel Glass, Ed Davidowitz, Mel Stein, Lenny Sandler, Bob Burstein, Frank Hogan, Dick Nachman, myself, Jim Yeargin, Irving Lang, John Keenan, Larry Bernstein, Sam Fierro, and Burt Roberts.

I couldn't get out the name Frank! *Everyone* called him Mr. Hogan, and I never addressed him in any other way in all the years I knew him. I don't know of anyone else who did, except Al Scotti, his longtime chief assistant district attorney and the chief of the Rackets Bureau, who called him "Chief."

Mr. Hogan died in 1974. I attended his wake at Campbell's Funeral Parlor, where Uncle Tom had been waked. *Everyone* came and paid their respects. His overflowing funeral Mass was said at the Church of St. Ignatius Loyola, just a few blocks from Campbell's, on the Upper East Side of Manhattan. The counsel and advice as well as the opportunities he had afforded me after I had left his office were incredible, and when his casket passed the pew in which I was seated, I knew that I had lost another champion.

7

Robinson, Silverman, Pearce and Aronsohn

ON APRIL 1, 1964, a little more than a year after my uncle Tom's death, I left Hogan's office to join the firm of Robinson, Silverman, Pearce and Aronsohn. I did so with a heavy heart. Hogan had imbued me with the importance of public service, and as far as I was concerned, he was the best.

But family obligations, financial or otherwise, must always come first. Allen Schwartz, my friend and former colleague at Hogan's office, had a friend by the name of Eddie Schoen at the firm of Robinson, Silverman, Pearce and Aronsohn, where he was a highly regarded real-estate associate. When Eddie told Allen that his firm was interested in hiring an associate who would be primarily involved in labor law on the union side, Allen recommended me. Although I had no background in labor law, I applied for the job. My interest in representing working men and women was the continuing influence of my father.

I was hired—the eighth lawyer to join the firm—and I've been there ever since. I became a partner in 1968 and a managing partner in 1978. Over the years we became a firm 180 lawyers, due in the main to the extraordinary leadership of my partner and friend Mike Rosen. Joining the firm was the best professional decision I ever made. Effective July 1, 2002, we merged with the St. Louis-based firm of Bryan Cave LLP. As a result we now have 850 lawyers and offices throughout the United States and overseas. The merger was a superb move for a host of reasons.

During my early days, I immersed myself in the study of labor law. I worked with Matty Silverman, who was a partner in the firm and soon became my mentor. We were to work together on a daily basis for twenty-four years.

One of our clients was Local One of the Amalgamated Lithographers of America. The lithographic printing process begins with a lithographic camera, which is operated by a highly skilled camera operator. The film produced by the lithographic camera is cut and positioned by a "stripper"; a lithographic plate is then made from the film by a lithographic platemaker and placed on a lithographic press that is operated by lithographic press operators. The process requires a separate plate for each color (red, blue, yellow, black), and each plate must be perfectly synchronized on the press in order to create a clear image.

The lithographic plate is chemically treated so that the printing surface absorbs ink and repels water while the nonprinting surface does the opposite. The printing surface does not touch the paper directly but rather transfers the image onto a "blanket" that in turn makes contact with the paper. Thus the term *offset* printing is commonly used to describe the lithographic process. But I've probably told you more about lithography than you ever wanted to know.[1]

For years, Matty and I worked zealously to protect the legal integrity of that process as a separate and distinct collective-bargaining unit in the courts and before the National Labor Relations Board (NLRB). Without such recognition, lithographic unions would have been swallowed by larger unions because, in many shops, the lithographic unit constituted a small percentage of the overall workforce.

In 1968, we took on the legal representation of the United Furniture Workers of America, a relatively small international union with a membership of about 35,000. The industry's wages were low, and accordingly we knew that our fees would not compensate us for the time we expended. Nonetheless, I prevailed upon our senior partner, Ben Robinson, to allow me to represent the Furniture Workers with the understanding that I would carry out all of my other duties as well—my first major client.

In those days, I used to say that man for man, pound for pound, the Furniture Workers were the most effective and toughest labor organizers in the United States. They organized in the Deep South, where the bulk of the furniture industry was located. They organized the American Tent Company in Canton, Mississippi, where the workforce was composed almost exclusively of black

---

[1] Technology has since changed lithography dramatically.

women—a daunting task at the time, but they did it! They also organized the Memphis Chair Company in Memphis, Tennessee, again an all-black workforce and another almost impossible task— but they did it. In 1970, the Furniture Workers took on the organization of the La-Z-Boy plant in Florence, South Carolina. The La-Z-Boy Chair Company was viciously anti-union, and it was a brutal campaign. Not only did I represent the Furniture Workers before the NLRB and in the courts, but I walked the picket line.

The president of the Furniture Workers at the time was Fred Fulford, and he was a firebrand. While the strike at Florence was effective, the company had substantial inventory stored in a warehouse and continued to supply its customers. Fred told me of his intention to picket the warehouse and close it down. I advised him that such a picket line would be illegal and that the union could be required to pay substantial damages because other parties used that warehouse. A short time later he called me and said, "Jim, I appreciate your advice, and I know you're right—but I'm going to picket that warehouse starting tomorrow morning." And he did. Shortly thereafter, the company capitulated and the Furniture Workers got a contract. So much for lawyer's advice!

Shortly after we took on the representation of the Furniture Workers, we were afforded an opportunity to represent the International Typographical Union (ITU) Negotiated Pension Plan. The ITU dates back to 1850 and is the oldest trade union in the United States. The ITU represented employees engaged in the printing trade, particularly employees employed by newspapers across the country. The hallmarks of the ITU were militancy and intelligence, and it was highly respected within the trade union movement.

When we first got involved with the ITU Negotiated Pension Plan, the international president of the ITU was Elmer Brown, one of the most distinguished labor leaders in the history of the trade union movement. Brown's power over the newspaper industry at the time was awesome. Up to then, there had been no national ITU pension plan; each newspaper had its own pension plan. Brown wanted to establish a national plan for a number of reasons.

He wanted to provide his membership (approximately 110,000 members) with portability, that is to say, he wanted to give his

Addressing the Furniture Workers Convention in Memphis in 1972. Seated, from left: Leroy Clark, vice president; Carl Scarbrough, secretary treasurer; and Fred Fulford, president.

members an opportunity to move from one employer to another and still be able to continue their pension fund credits. He also recognized that a national pension plan would be far more stable financially in that it would not be dependent on any one employer or on any one city or region. Finally, he recognized that such a plan would have more investment strength.

One of the underlying concepts of Brown's national pension plan was that it was structured in such a way that the pension plans of the various employers, and particularly the newspapers across the country, could merge into it. The basic idea was to create a "tent" under which everybody would be able to gather. It was a unique and unprecedented concept. Matty and I drafted the original documents establishing the plan.

The ITU Negotiated Pension Plan was launched, and everything we hoped for and anticipated took place. Most of the newspaper pension plans established for the printers and others in related trades merged into the ITU Negotiated Pension Plan. I can remember the early days when the union had to put forth seed money to get the ITU Negotiated Pension Plan underway. It was a struggle, but I am pleased to report that under the leadership of the current chairman, Bill Boarman, the ITU Negotiated Pension Plan has assets in excess of a billion dollars, provides retirement with dignity for thousands of workers, and will continue to do so for decades to come.

Nowadays I spend most of my time with other lawyers, bankers, corporate executives, elected officials, real estate developers, stockbrokers, and other "masters of the universe," and that's fine. But I always look forward to, relish, and cherish my time with my union clients. I love being with working people. They are the best. Not all of them, of course, but most of them. They're dedicated, they're savvy, they're straight, they have no hidden agendas, and they appreciate what you do for them. I share that great joy with my partner and friend Andy Irving, who mirrors Matty Silverman in so many ways.

César Chávez

One of the high points of my legal career was working with César Chávez, who in my opinion was one of the great heroes of the twentieth century. Against incredible odds, he organized migrant workers in California, Arizona, and Florida.

Fruits and vegetables must be harvested and delivered before they spoil. Accordingly, seasonal harvest crews are on the scene for relatively short periods of time, after which they move on to other farms. The transient nature of farm work makes it almost impossible to organize farm workers. For generations, growers had absolute control over the field workforce. Workers lived in constant fear and were paid a pittance. Working conditions were atrocious, and living conditions were abominable. Most said it couldn't be done. And then along came César Chávez, who said: *"Sí, se puede"*—"Yes, it can"—and he did it!

Chávez adhered to the principles of nonviolent resistance as practiced by Mahatma Gandhi and Martin Luther King Jr. His entire life was devoted to "La Causa." Again and again, he went on hunger strikes to rally support for his cause. He preached the social values espoused by the Catholic Church and was Christ-like in his manner. When faced with violence at the hands of anti-union thugs, he turned the other cheek. By force of his dogged determination, his personal demeanor, and his phenomenal leadership abilities, more than fifty thousand laborers joined the ranks of the United Farm Workers (UFW). Under his leadership, the hiring hall of the UFW replaced the dreaded job boss, hourly rates increased steadily, and farm workers were afforded health and welfare coverage for the first time. People who had lived in squalor were enjoying substantially better living conditions, though they were still poor.

In the early 1970s, the major growers were anxious to get rid of César Chávez and the UFW, and started to sign "sweetheart" contracts with the Teamsters. In response, Chávez launched a nationwide boycott of grapes, lettuce, and Gallo wine. I had been following Chávez's career closely and admired him greatly. When the UFW boycott campaign commenced in New York, I called Chávez at his headquarters in California. I told him that I was a young labor lawyer representing unions and their related funds, and that I would be willing to represent the UFW without charge in connection with his boycott campaign in New York. I had no idea what I was letting myself and our law firm in for, but I'm glad and proud that I did it.

For the next several years, our firm was involved in representing the UFW on various fronts. Working on behalf of the UFW was awe-inspiring and one of the great joys of my professional life.

The UFW picketed New York–area stores that engaged in the sale of grapes and lettuce picked by non-UFW workers. They also picketed stores that were selling Gallo wine. When the UFW put up a picket line, they didn't just stand around holding signs and mouthing slogans. Sometimes fights would break out with persons crossing the picket line, and we would find ourselves in criminal court defending representatives of the UFW against charges of assault. Store owners frequently sought injunctions against the UFW's almost impenetrable picket lines, and we would go to court to resist those injunctions. In addition, we registered the black eagle as the official symbol of the UFW in

New York State so that stores using the black eagle wrongfully would be subject to criminal penalties.

The nationwide boycott launched by César Chávez was enormously successful. In addition, the State of California, under the leadership of Governor Jerry Brown, enacted legislation that provided for fair and honest elections in connection with efforts to organize growers in California, to the distinct advantage of the UFW.

Joan Crawford

As time passed, I became involved in litigation that was non–union related. One memorable case had to do with the estate of Joan Crawford, the great actress who won an Academy Award for her role in *Mildred Pierce* (1945) and was nominated for an Academy Award for her performances in *Possessed* (1947) and *Sudden Fear* (1952).

Joan Crawford died on May 10, 1977, at the age of sixty-nine. She left behind four adopted children: Christina, Christopher, Cathy, and Cindy. Under the terms of her will, she bequeathed most of her property to charities.

She left substantial sums of money to Cathy and Cindy, but she disinherited Christina and Christopher. Consequently, Christina and Christopher contested the will, with Christina leading the charge.

I never met Ms. Crawford, but one of my law partners was a friend of hers and was the executor of her estate. Consequently our firm represented her estate, and I was put in charge of all of the resulting litigation.

The legal question was whether Ms. Crawford had "testamentary capacity." The law in that regard is straightforward and relatively simple. Did Ms. Crawford, at the time she executed her will, know generally the nature and extent of her holdings and the "natural objects of her bounty"? And was the execution of her will a voluntary act on her part, or was she "unduly influenced" by another person or persons?

I read up on the much-chronicled Joan Crawford and deposed Christina and Christopher. I interviewed Cathy and Cindy, their spouses, and dozens of Ms. Crawford's friends, colleagues, and employees. I talked to the witnesses who had been present when Ms. Crawford officially executed her will, on October 28, 1976, at her home on East 69th Street in New York City.

There was no question whatever about the fact that Ms. Crawford had "testamentary capacity" at the time she executed her will. She had disinherited Christina and Christopher because her relationships with both of them had been disastrous.

Ms. Crawford was a strict disciplinarian and a perfectionist. Those qualities had helped propel her to stardom. Consequently, she tried to instill those same qualities in her adopted children. In so doing, she was, I'm sure, a demanding parent. But she wasn't the only one to blame for the breakdown in her relationships with Christina and Christopher. Christina had defied her mother again and again, had disappointed her constantly, and had disparaged her publicly. Christopher had proved to be a great disappointment as well, though he had been far less willful and deliberate than Christina in his relationship with his mother.

Neither Christina nor Christopher had seen or spoken to their mother in the last years of her life. In fact, Ms. Crawford had disinherited Christina and Christopher in previous wills, so that even if they could convince the court to set aside the final will, it would profit them nothing! Their objections to the October 28, 1976 will included an allegation that Ms. Crawford was of "unsound mind" when she executed the will. There were references to her drinking and to the fact that she had cancer and refused to be treated because she was a Christian Scientist. There were charges that she had become a recluse in her final years. And there were allegations that Cathy and her husband, Jerome LaLonde, had "unduly influenced" Ms. Crawford. There were other "throw-ins," such as that she was of "unsound mind" because she was meticulous and concerned about security!

I went about ascertaining the facts. I found no psychological or psychiatric evidence that Joan was of "unsound mind" on the day she executed her will, or at any other time. Joan did like her gin, and at one point she had been a heavy drinker, but she hadn't taken a drink for almost a year prior to the execution of her will. Joan had cancer of the rectum and had refused treatment, but not because she was a Christian Scientist. She simply preferred not to go through the pain and suffering of surgery and chemotherapy.

More importantly, she was an extremely proud woman and did not want to become a public spectacle in a hospital with tubes and other medical paraphernalia intruding into various parts of her body. She was not a recluse in the "Howard Hughes" sense, as suggested by Christina; rather, she kept to her apartment because she was ill and didn't look well. She wanted to be remembered as she had been in her prime. The suggestions that she was mentally unbalanced because she was meticulous and security-conscious struck me as patently absurd, and the notion that Cathy and Jerome LaLonde, or anyone else, could have imposed their wills upon someone as strong-minded as Joan Crawford also struck me as ridiculous. The strength of Joan Crawford's will was the stuff of legend.

After I took the depositions of Christina and Christopher, I began feeling sorry for Christopher, because he struck me as the unwitting tool of his manipulative and calculating older sister. After the depositions, Christina realized that her case was going nowhere, and she offered to settle for a piddling sum that I, in good conscience, had to accept since our legal fees would have greatly exceeded the offer if we had refused it and gone to trial.

In retrospect, Christina's lawsuit seems to have been little more than a springboard for her memoir *Mommie Dearest*. She had signed with the prominent William Morris Agency, and throughout the litigation she was feverishly involved in writing that book, which portrayed her mother as the worst bitch and the most horrible mother that ever lived. *Mommie Dearest* went on to be a best seller and a movie that did extremely well at the box office. Needless to say, Christina fared very well financially.

The legacy of *Mommie Dearest* is that Joan Crawford will probably be remembered in large measure as Christina portrayed her, and that strikes me as wrong and terribly sad. There are invariably two sides to every story. I also think that children who publicly disparage their parents, particularly after they are dead and can't respond, are despicable.

Josef Begun

In the fall of 1982, Zeesy Schnur, the executive director of the Committee for the Relief of Soviet Jewry, asked me to go to the Soviet Union to aid the cause of one Josef Begun.

At that time, the Cold War between the Soviet Union and the United States was at its coldest. Russian fighter pilots had just shot down a Korean civilian passenger plane over Sakhalin Island, killing all aboard, and President Reagan had recently referred to the Soviet Union as the "Evil Empire."

Zeesy told me that I could choose another lawyer to accompany me, so I chose Bob Donnelly, my old friend from the Hogan days. The Committee had decided that non-Jewish lawyers would be more effective than the Jewish lawyers who had been sent there previously. After many briefings, we flew to Moscow in early December.

Josef Begun was a "refusnik," that is to say, a Russian citizen who had applied to emigrate to Israel and had been refused. Such conduct was regarded as disloyalty, and as a result the Soviet state fired him from his job and charged him with "parasitism," that is, failing to make a contribution to the Soviet Union. (The fact that the state was the sole employer in the Soviet Union was not taken into account in connection with the crime of "parasitism.") While he was awaiting trial, he taught Jewish culture to Russian Jews. His apartment was raided during one of his lectures, his teaching materials were confiscated, and he was charged with the additional crime of "slandering the Soviet Union."[2] He was convicted of both crimes and was sentenced to a substantial jail term in Siberia. In addition, while incarcerated he did not cooperate with jail authorities as demanded, and accordingly the person in charge of the prison gave him additional time, as he was empowered to do under existing Soviet law, without a hearing. Our job was to do everything we could for Begun.

Moscow was awful. It was freezing cold and buried in snow. It was dimly lit both outside and in the hotel. The food was the worst. We were told that our rooms would be bugged—and that we might well be followed by the KGB. We were also instructed only to use public phones outside of the hotel. Because all of the state's money and brainpower went into weaponry, the vast majority of its people lived in poverty and misery. The merchandise available for purchase was third-rate and overpriced.

---

[2] At that time, the Soviet state was supreme and there were *no* individual or religious rights.

The black market was flourishing and alcoholism was rampant. We found that many of the Russians who lived in Moscow did not drink socially but rather in order to pass out. Crime was everywhere, and we were urged not to leave the hotel at night. When we did leave our rooms, we were required to leave our keys with one of the matrons who were stationed on every floor, twenty-four hours a day—which, of course, facilitated searches of our rooms when we were not there. Our daily food consisted of, for lack of other edible items, brown bread, hard-boiled eggs, caviar, and ice cream. The caviar and the ice cream were delicious, but you can only eat so much.

The first thing we did on arrival was to check in with the U.S. Embassy. When we arrived, we were ushered into the so-called "safe room" and told, to our amazement, that we should assume that the rest of the embassy was "insecure."

We kept the embassy aware of our activities and went there for some good American food like hamburgers, hot dogs, and pizzas, and to attend Mass on Sundays. (Religion, of course, was banned in the Soviet Union.)

After checking in at the embassy, we visited with Begun's long-time female companion and Begun's son who lived with her, and later with other Russian Jews we had been told to contact. Getting around Moscow was a serious challenge, but we managed. We learned that prison authorities had blocked the mail and the monthly food and clothing allotments Begun's relatives and friends had been sending him. We learned that as a result, he had concluded that he had been abandoned by everyone and was in a state of deep depression.

We began efforts to contact Soviet officials on Begun's behalf. We had letters of introduction from Mayor Ed Koch of New York, who had recently been highly complimentary of Moscow's subway system,[3] Senator Ted Kennedy, and Mario Cuomo, the newly elected governor of New York.

---

[3] The Moscow subways are much farther below the surface than New York City's because they must get below the tundra, and the escalators that serve them are unbelievably efficient. The stations are decorated with wonderful mosaics and are squeaky clean. The trains are on time and immaculate. No one on the train talks, and adults give up their seats to children, children being honored generally because of their potential.

We were told that the most effective card would be Cuomo's, because the Russians are long-term in their approach and regarded Cuomo as a prospect for the future. While the advice as to Cuomo proved correct, all of our efforts to visit Begun, and to have him released or his sentence reduced, failed.

We did, however, prevail upon the authorities to give Begun his mail and his monthly food and clothing allowances from relatives and friends. The authorities also allowed him to marry his longtime companion, albeit in jail. We were also helpful in getting Vladimir Petroff to represent Begun in the courts. The good news was that Petroff was the best criminal lawyer in the Soviet Union. The bad news was that in the history of the Soviet Union, no one charged with a political crime had ever been acquitted—and no such conviction had ever been overturned on appeal! That record remained in place despite Petroff's efforts on behalf of Begun.

Bob and I felt that we had accomplished very little. But we were assured by one and all that we had accomplished a great deal by conveying to Begun the knowledge that there were still people who cared about him. We were told that we had given him renewed hope and that our trip to Moscow had given solace and encouragement to other refusniks as well. Even in the face of the most daunting odds, you've got to give it your best shot because you never know what may result. James and Gillian, never be afraid to dream Don Quixote's "impossible dream."

I tried to keep in touch with Begun's wife and son, but with limited success. Finally we learned that Begun had been released and had joined his wife and son in Israel. When I received that information, I was moved.

Bob and I got home just in time for Christmas. I was never so happy to get home. Ever since then, I have had a much deeper appreciation of what our country is all about.

Matty Silverman died on July 8, 1988. I delivered his eulogy at the Yale Club on October 12, 1988. Excerpts from that eulogy can be found in appendix B.

8

The Gill Commission

IN DECEMBER 1988, Edward I. Koch, the mayor of New York, asked me to chair a commission to investigate corruption and mismanagement within the New York City school system. I had been introduced to Ed many years before by Allen Schwartz and had been involved in all of Ed's previous mayoral campaigns.

I agreed to the assignment under three conditions: that my friend Paul Curran serve on the commission; that the commission receive sufficient funding; and that I be given a free hand with respect to hiring of staff.

The mayor promised sufficient funding and assured me that I would have a free hand selecting the staff. But he expressed some hesitation over the appointment of Curran. I said, "Mayor, if I don't get Curran, you don't get me," and he acquiesced.

I insisted on Curran for a number of reasons. First, I didn't know any of the other members of the commission whom Koch had already appointed. Second, Paul had served as the chairman of the State Investigation Commission under Governor Rockefeller; he had been the U.S. attorney for the Southern District of New York under Presidents Nixon and Ford; and he had been appointed by Griffin Bell, the attorney general during the Carter administration, to investigate the operations of the Carter peanut farm. He had served in all of those capacities magnificently and with independence, professionalism, and integrity. I wanted his expertise and his judgment. I knew, of course, that I would have his loyalty.

The first task was to put a team on the field. For executive director and general counsel, I chose Austin V. Campriello, a former chief of the Rackets Bureau in district attorney Bob Morgenthau's office. After consulting with Austin and others, I chose Joe Comperiati, a former deputy inspector for the New York Police Department, as chief investigator. They, in turn, were empowered to hire lawyers, investigators, and accountants as needed to carry out our mission.

I also hired Tracey Gibbons, whom I had known since her childhood, and Jennifer Cunningham, a Root Tilden Scholar at NYU Law School. Gibbons was an administrative wizard with a rare capacity for cutting through red tape, and she always left them smiling. Cunningham was and is a bloody genius, and she did virtually everything for us. The other major players were Amy Jane Rettew, a brilliant young lawyer recommended by Austin and borrowed from Bob Morgenthau's Appeals Bureau, and our chief investigatory accountant, Frank Frattolillio, borrowed from the Feds pursuant to a statute that allowed us to do so without having to pay his salary.

Through the good offices of my friend Dick Condon, who was then the first deputy police commissioner, we borrowed police officers from the New York City Police Department Intelligence Unit (without having to pay them, either), including some very young-looking officers whom we registered as high school students for undercover purposes. We also borrowed other accountants from the Feds in addition to Frank Frattolillio.

As soon as a skeleton team was in place, I visited Judge Whitman Knapp, the former chairman of the Knapp Commission, which had exposed widespread and systemic corruption within the New York Police Department in the 1970s. Knapp is a delightful, charming man with a delicious self-deprecating sense of humor. He conducts his life in the way he thinks it ought to be conducted, without reference to how other people think he ought to do so. I am extremely fond of him, and his advice was very helpful. The advice that I remember most clearly was his advice to be patient. He said that it would take time before our commission could get up and running and win the confidence of the people in the system. And indeed, during our first several months Austin would come to me and say, "Chief, nothing is happening, I'm concerned," and I would turn to him and say, wisely, "Austin, not to worry, it will happen." And it did.

Our commission was officially known as the Joint Commission on Integrity in the Public Schools, "Joint" because it was cosponsored by the City of New York and the Board of Education. So I called upon Bobby Wagner, then president of the Board of Education. We had a pleasant and fruitful meeting. He promised to cooperate in every respect, and he did so.

Austin and I met with the chancellor of the Board of Education, Joseph Fernandez, to elicit his cooperation and assure him that when we were about to take public action, we would brief him beforehand, so that he would be in a position to deal with his community and the media. I also met with Sandy Feldman, the president of the teachers union, and gave her similar assurances.

The last person that I met with before fully launching our investigation was His Eminence John Cardinal O'Connor, the archbishop of New York. The meeting was held at his residence and was scheduled to last for a half hour. I sought his counsel because I was aware that many of the children in New York's public school system are Catholics. Moreover, he had shown an abiding interest in the welfare of public school students of *all* faiths. Towards the end of our meeting, which lasted more than an hour, he asked me how many children were in the public school system. I told him there were approximately one million. He said, "We have approximately a hundred thousand children in the archdiocesan schools in the inner city. That makes us one-tenth your size. In our central office, we have approximately fifty employees, so I would assume you have something in the area of five hundred employees, perhaps even more by virtue of the fact that you have special education and other things we don't have."

I replied, "Your eminence, we really don't know, but we think we have somewhere between 6,500 and 7,000 employees in the central office."

He said to me, "James, you don't need me—you need an accounting firm!"

How right he was. The staff of the Board of Education was then, and still is, bloated beyond belief. There is layer upon layer; there are button-pushers on top of button-pushers. And it's impenetrable. It's become a way of life, and it's a disgrace. This explains in large measure the board's ineptness and incompetence, and why the cost of educating a student in the public school system is more than twice that of educating a student in the inner-city archdiocesan parochial system, which provides a vastly superior education. An *enormous* reduction of Board of Education employees is long overdue!

In 1988, Matthew Barnwell, the principal of PS 53 in the Bronx, was caught buying crack from a dealer on a Harlem street. Police officers had staked out the dealer, and they arrested Barnwell without knowing who he was. That arrest gave rise to what the media would quickly label the Gill Commission. We learned that reliable sources had supplied damaging information concerning Barnwell to the office of the inspector general of the Board of Education a year before his arrest. At the time, the inspector general's office was headed by Michael Sofarelli.

Austin Campriello embarked upon a case study as to how the office of the inspector general had conducted its investigation of Barnwell. He also did a study of how Sofarelli's office had conducted an investigation into nonexistent courses that had purportedly been taught at Stevenson High School. These two case studies established that Sofarelli's office had squandered its considerable resources on trivial matters instead of focusing on significant illicit activities.

Public hearings were conducted, and the results of our investigation were included in a report entitled "Investigating the Investigators," filed with David Dinkins (who by this time had succeeded Ed Koch as mayor of New York), Robert Wagner, and Joseph Fernandez, on March 15, 1990.

The commission recommended that the office of inspector general of the New York City Board of Education be eliminated and replaced by an independent investigatory unit fashioned in the same manner as the Gill Commission. The recommendations were followed, and that unit is still in place today. It was headed by Edward Stancik, former deputy chief of the Rackets Bureau under District Attorney Robert Morgenthau until Stancik's death in March 2002.[1]

We recommended that the investigatory unit not be answerable to the chancellor or to the Board of Education but to the office

---

[1] On June 18, 2002, Commissioner Rose Gill Hearn of the Department of Investigation appointed former police commissioner Richard Condon to replace Stancik, effective July 1, 2002.

of the Department of Investigation of the City of New York. The office was created by an executive order signed by Mayor Dinkins. We also recommended that the unit be provided with effective tools to deal with crime and inefficiency within the New York City school system: the power to issue subpoenas, to take testimony under oath, and to grant immunity.

When Stancik issued reports, he was sometimes charged with playing to the media to advance his own career. During the days of the Gill Commission we conducted public hearings, held press conferences, issued press releases, and filed two comprehensive reports. Meaningful changes in the public school system will not take place unless there is a sustained sense of public outrage! That's why public attention is essential. I understood that, and so did Stancik!

Much of what the Gill Commission found was infuriating. But perhaps the most exasperating matter was the hiring of Frank Carr.

In February 1989, Frank Carr applied to teach at JHS 22 in the Bronx. He was hired despite a record of nine arrests and three convictions, including a Connecticut conviction for sexual assault of a female student and a pending New Jersey indictment for molesting two female school children. Carr lied on his application to hide his prior arrests and convictions, claiming that he had never been arrested or convicted of any crime. At no time did the Board of Investigators (the agency entrusted to do teachers' background checks) call either of the schools where Carr had taught, nor did it ask the New Jersey or the Connecticut state police whether Carr had a criminal record.

Instead the Board of Examiners simply sent fingerprints to New York State and the FBI. Because all of his arrests and convictions were outside the State of New York, the state police report showed no record.

Stephen Conboy, the chief investigator for the Board of Examiners, acknowledged that FBI reports do not come back for at least six months and sometimes longer. He also admitted that "out-of-state teachers" were hired before the Board of Examiners received the FBI report. This meant, of course, that a teacher from outside New York who was a child molester or any other type of criminal could operate in the school system for a minimum of six months without fear of detection.

I had the following exchange with Mr. Conboy on that subject during a pubic hearing:

> CHAIRMAN GILL: I have the impression that Jack the Ripper could get through that system, from listening to your testimony. That is my feeling. I mean, if somebody comes in from out of state, with a record as long as your arm, and brings with him some bogus documents from schools that he supposedly taught at, and nothing comes back from New York State with respect to a record, he gets in for at least six or seven months, until the FBI catches up; yes?
>
> STEPHEN CONBOY [chief investigator for the Board of Examiners]: Yes, that is correct.
>
> GILL: Is that appalling to you?
>
> CONBOY: Yes, it is.

Apparently not so *appalling* that he ever did anything about it!

But it was even worse. Since 1974, the Code of Federal Regulations had prohibited the FBI from releasing information to a civilian agency like the Board of Examiners, except where there had been a disposition or when the case was less than one year old. Incredibly, the Board of Examiners was totally unaware of that and thought that when they got a report from the FBI it included everything! Indeed, the board had operated under that mistaken impression until informed that such was not the case by Austin Campriello in 1989! On that subject, the following exchange took place:

> CHAIRMAN GILL: When did you find out, for the first time, that you weren't getting arrest information from the FBI that was more than a year old?
>
> CONBOY: When Mr. Campriello and I met in November of 1989.
>
> GILL: So you were in the dark from 1974 until you met with Mr. Campriello [in 1989], is that right?
>
> CONBOY: Yes. . . .
>
> COMMISSIONER CURRAN: You just assumed the FBI record was complete?
>
> CONBOY: Yes.

And so when the FBI report finally came in on Carr, it was tragically incomplete. Had the board made inquiry with respect to the breach of the peace conviction in Connecticut *eventually* reported by the FBI, it would have found that it involved sexual molestation of a female student. Had the board checked Carr's credentials with the Connecticut school he had taught at, it would have found the truth. Had the board checked his credentials with the New Jersey school he had taught at, it would have found that he was under indictment for sexual molestation of two female students. Nor was the board distressed or disturbed when it learned that Carr had lied on his application, saying that he had not been convicted, when in fact he had been, as indicated by the FBI report!

As a result of this gross incompetence and mind-boggling indifference, William Green, the principal of JHS 22 in the Bronx, was able to hire his old friend Frank Carr. Shortly after Carr arrived at JHS 22, he was at it again! Because of the incredible ineptitude of the Board of Examiners, two more girls were molested in a stairwell at JHS 22! That was then and remains an outrage!

I presented the evidence against Carr to the office of the district attorney of the Bronx, Robert Johnson. He conducted an investigation and sided with Carr's contention that he had simply "hugged" the two girls. Johnson had just been elected at the time, and I think that with the passage of time, he has become more seasoned and is less sensitive about outsiders uncovering criminal conduct on his turf.

Since Carr had filed his application for employment in Brooklyn, wherein he lied under penalty of perjury relative to the fact that he had never been convicted, we asked the district attorney of Brooklyn to take appropriate criminal action, and he did. Carr was arrested at JHS 22 and later pleaded guilty. Later the two Bronx girls testified against Carr in the case in New Jersey. Carr interposed his standard defense that what he had done to the two New Jersey girls was nothing more than a hug. Thanks in large measure to the testimony of the two incredibly courageous girls from the Bronx, Carr was convicted.

When we conducted public hearings with respect to the Carr affair, I was beset by the press during a break. They wanted to know why Carr hadn't been arrested in the Bronx for molesting the two girls. I told them they'd have to talk to the district attorney of Bronx County to ascertain the answer to that question.

Later one of the reporters approached me and said that he had been in touch with the office of the district attorney of Bronx County and was told that there had been an investigation with respect to the matter, that a conclusion had been reached, and that what Carr did to those two girls was nothing more than a hug. I saw red and responded: "If that bird 'hugged' my daughter the way he 'hugged' those two girls, I would personally shoot him between the eyes with a gun."

I was praised and criticized by friend and foe alike for making that statement, but I'm glad I did so and I'd say it again. I was furious about what Carr had done to those two girls in the Bronx, and I wanted to let him know, in no uncertain terms, that he wasn't "bullshitting" me!

There are thirty-five school districts in the New York City system, each of which is headed by a superintendent. District 27 is geographically the largest of the school districts, and covers a large part of Queens, Woodhaven, Richmond Hill, Ozone Park, Jamaica, Howard Beach, Broad Channel, and the Rockaways. With approximately 29,000 students, it has the fourth-largest student population in the city.

In 1986, Colman Genn became the superintendent of District 27. Shortly after he was hired, several members of the community school board, which had hired him, made it clear that if he did not do their bidding in terms of hiring, his own job would be in jeopardy.

A Gill Commission public hearing conducted at the New York County Lawyers Association building on Vesey Street. From left to right: Paul Curran, myself, and Austin Campriello.

Colman Genn is a very decent man and was tormented by the fact that the school board members were hiring and promoting unqualified applicants. In late 1988, he learned about the formation of the Gill Commission and considered coming to us for help. His wife had a cousin who worked for Amy Jane Rettew in Robert Morgenthau's office, and when Genn's cousin learned that Rettew was joining the Gill Commission, she reported that fact to Genn.

Genn came to the Commission in January 1989. We persuaded him to wear a wire and surreptitiously record conversations with the school board members who were putting pressure on him. One of our staff detectives, John O'Rourke, was assigned to help Genn, and the two worked closely together for several months.

The conversations Colman Genn recorded were horrifying. They demonstrated beyond doubt that Community School District 27 was nothing more than a patronage trough. Not once did we hear a single conversation by the school board members concerning education or the children! *All* conversation centered on jobs—what jobs were available; how much they paid; who should get them. Nor was there any conversation about the qualifications of the proposed candidates, most of whom were relatives, friends, or political cronies. Racial, ethnic, and religious biases were commonplace. And time and again, Genn was threatened with the loss of his job if he didn't deliver on the board's demands.

Genn testified at public hearings, and his tapes were played. It was a gross spectacle, so raw that the entire city was shocked. Two of the board members, James C. Sullivan and Samuel Granirer, were indicted on felony charges by the district attorney of Queens County and the U.S. attorney for the Eastern District of New York. Both pleaded guilty to charges of coercion and mail fraud.

Superintendents of two other districts, Lavander Lilly of District 19 and Marco Hernandez of District 32, came to us with similar reports about their districts. It became apparent that the problem was widespread: by and large, the community school boards had replaced the local political clubs as patronage troughs!

In early 1990, the Colman Genn story was told on *60 Minutes,* and the nation was shocked. In April 1990 the Gill Commission had recommended that the hiring authority of local school boards be curtailed and that superintendents be protected against the demands of grasping, avaricious community school board members.

But despite all of our efforts, no remedial action was taken until 1997, when Governor Pataki signed a bill that finally took local school boards out of the patronage business. I attended the signing ceremony at Stuyvesant High School in Lower Manhattan, and Governor Pataki kindly gave me one of the pens he used to sign the bill into law. It is among my most treasured possessions.

Community school board elections are held in May, rather than in November when other elections are held. As a result, there is a relatively sparse turnout. In addition, *proportional voting* is utilized—that is, if there are several openings, the voters are asked to rank the candidates in order of their preference. Many voters don't understand the concept of proportional voting. Moreover, the elections still use paper ballots, which are subject to substantial fraud at the time of the count. But most importantly, the Board of Elections and the Board of Education have totally failed to safeguard the integrity of those elections at the registration stage. Parents of school-age children are eligible to vote in community school board elections, but only once. That requires that the Board of Education certify bona fide parent voters to the Board of Elections, and requires the Board of Elections to ensure against other forms of parent-voter fraud. *Both* simply ignore their duties and responsibilities imposed upon them by law! It's amazing! As a result, those elections have been open to wholesale election fraud!

In order to demonstrate the point, we had one of our investigators vote as a parent-voter thirty-three times in two school districts in the school board elections of 1989! Bogus registration papers were filed and approved in each case. Not a single set of bogus registration papers were detected or turned down! Because voter turnout is small and the margin of victory is so slim, God knows how many such elections have been stolen by this method.

In a public hearing, Lawrence E. Becker, counsel to Chancellor Fernandez, tried to explain away the Board of Education's failure by saying that there was concern that safeguards against election

Bill-signing ceremony at Stuyvesant High School in Battery Park City, Governor Pataki, et al.

fraud would *discourage voter turnout!* A mind-boggling statement—and an obvious cop-out.

Aaron Maslow, the general counsel to the Board of Elections, suggested in his testimony that the board is accustomed to dealing with larger turnouts in regular elections and views the school-board elections as a small and unimportant part of its job. The underlying inertia was perhaps best expressed in Maslow's statement to representatives of the Gill Commission: "We don't have anything at all to do with the schools, we just run the election."

The Gill Commission recommended to the state legislature that school-board elections be held in November, with the regular elections; that paper ballots and proportional balloting be eliminated; and that voting machines be used in connection with school-board elections. No such action has been taken. Moreover, the commission was assured by both the Board of Elections and the Board of Education that corrective steps would be taken with respect to school-board elections. And yet in the elections of 1993, one of Stancik's investigators was able to vote as the same parent-voter fifteen times, and another investigator voted as a parent-voter ten times.

In an effort to address the fiscal irresponsibility that was distressingly rampant in the school system, our staff looked into the finances of several districts, and as expected, the results were appalling. For example, our investigation disclosed that there were no effective controls in place with respect to telephone calls, and that tens of thousands of dollars had been paid for long distance calls, overseas calls, collect calls, and third-party calls that were clearly personal in nature and unrelated to school business.

Between January 1988 and September 1989, Districts 4 and 9 spent $11,024.95 and $6,877.40, respectively, on so-called specialty calls, almost all of which were to porno lines. School employees were dialing "900" services like: "Hottest Adult Fantasies," "Cross-Dressing Line," "Hard Core Trivia Line," "City of Sluts," "The Skin Line," "Dial-a-Hunk," and "970-LUST." There were others with names so offensive that I would not print them here.

To our astonishment, Districts 4 and 9 *knew* all about their telephone problems and did *nothing* other than a few useless memos—even though all the "specialty" calls could have been stopped instantly with a simple request to the telephone company! Even worse, the Central Board knew about the situation, but they, too, did nothing except to write the usual memos, which were as ineffective as the ones written by the districts. In the meantime, the game continued—to the detriment of our children.

Eventually, the media got wind of our telephone disclosures. Some people were dismissed, others quit, and electronic blocks were, at long last, put in place.

After hearing Board of Ed Auditor General James Coney's testimony to the effect that the Central Board remained *paralyzed* in the face of the *most flagrant* fiscal abuses, we did simultaneous raids of seventeen of the thirty-five school districts in an effort to determine whether they had exercised appropriate fiscal responsibility with respect to computers and other expensive equipment. We found that 17 percent of the computers and 26 percent of the printers assigned to those seventeen school districts were unaccounted for. Further investigation revealed that much of that equipment had been stored for years and was unused, despite a crying need for such equipment. You can't make this stuff up! We concluded that Auditor General James Coney had been right on target when he testified unhesitatingly and unabashedly that there was no fiscal responsibility within the New York City school system!

Until recently, the Board of Education has consisted of seven members, two appointed by the mayor and the other five by each of the five borough presidents. Thus, no one was accountable, and that lack of accountability at the top permeated the entire institution. In the main, the Board was dysfunctional, ineffective, and incapable of dealing with the many and egregious problems facing the New York City school system.

In 1989, Mayor Koch and Mayor David Dinkins joined in the recommendations of our commission to give control of the Board of Education to the mayor of the City of New York—to no avail.[2]

I remember saying, in a fit of frustration at one of our public hearings, "The Board of Education is like a sleepy-eyed, lumbering brontosaurus, primarily interested in grazing." Members of the press wanted to know to whom I was referring specifically. I

---

[2] Mayor Rudy Giuliani also sought such control without success.

didn't answer at first, but when pressed, I responded in a fit of agitation: "Bobby Wagner, Bobby Wagner, Bobby Wagner, Bobby Wagner." As soon as the words were out of my mouth, I realized I had made a mistake. The next day, I received a call from Bobby Wagner, who asked me to lunch.

The day after that, I greeted Bobby in the lobby of the Yale Club. For the first time, and to my horror, I noticed a sleepy quality to his eyes. Over lunch, I apologized and explained that the press had goaded me into what I had said. It's not that I hadn't meant what I said about the Board of Education, and Wagner *was* its president, but Wagner was a good man—hard-working, conscientious, and well-intentioned—and he didn't deserve the treatment I had dealt him. I had crossed the line.

Some time later, after Wagner's death, I asked Ed Koch, who had been close to Bobby, whether Bobby had ever forgiven me. Ed told me that he had not.

In June 2002 Mayor Mike Bloomberg prevailed upon the New York State Legislature to give the mayor of the City of New York control over the Board of Education and the appointment of the chancellor. While that is a tremendous stride forward, it is only a beginning. The current system of education must be jettisoned and a new one put in its place. There is no way to fix the present structure. It must be redone from the ground up.

The top priority in the rebuilding of the New York City school system has to involve providing children who *want* to learn, who *want* to get an education, an environment in which they can receive one. Schoolroom discipline must be restored, and student uniforms should be made mandatory. Teachers and principals must have the authority to impose punishment for misbehavior. Habitual offenders should be subject to suspension, and incorrigibles should be transferred to a trade school operated by the Board of Education. Such schools should be geared to the business needs of the city, and the training should be first-rate. Students who wind up in a trade school should have the opportunity to return to an academic environment if they meet certain criteria, but if a student continues to be problematic in a trade school, he or she should be subject to removal from that school as well.

Students violating the ban on weapons or drugs should be dealt with swiftly and severely, as should anyone who threatens or intimidates another student.

The academic curriculum should be oriented toward college entrance. There should be a return to the fundamentals: reading, spelling, writing, arithmetic, the sciences, literature, grammar, languages, history, geography, and basic ethics and citizenship. There should be homework every night. There should be regular testing as well as final examinations. There should be no "social promotion" whatsoever—if the student doesn't make the grade, he or she should be kept back.

Slower-learning students should be placed in separate classes where the requirements are less stringent but where the courses are the same as those in the advanced group. Students should be transferred from one group to another on the basis of performance. Specially designed courses and schools should be available for gifted children and for those students who are *truly* learning-impaired.

Students who have no one to go home to when school lets out, such as those with single parents who work, should receive special consideration. Supervised after-school study halls and other activities should be available on the school premises. Special help should also be available to those students who are having difficulty with their studies or who wish to do better.

Teachers should be compensated on the basis of the performance of the students they teach. Tenure for teachers should not be automatic on the basis of the number of years taught; rather, efforts must be made to ensure that all teachers are conscientious and hard-working, and care about the children in their charge. Procedures to punish or remove teachers charged with misconduct or incompetence should be expedited. Neither justice nor fairness requires that such remedial procedures go on indefinitely. Indeed, such a factor is extremely detrimental to the system.

Under the new legislation, the Board of Education has an advisory role, and the chancellor is appointed by and answerable only to the mayor. Academic background should be taken into account in the selection of a chancellor but should not be a requirement.

The chancellor should have the right to hire and fire superintendents; superintendents should have the right to hire and fire principals; and principals should have the right to hire and fire teachers and their aides, as well as school custodians. Principals should have the right to set the hours when schools will be open. (Under the current system, those determinations are largely in the hands of the custodians, and that's absurd!)

Now all of that is a lot—and accomplishing it will take Herculean efforts on the part of many knowledgeable and strong-willed people—but it's the only way to correct what has been a governmental and educational tragedy of enormous proportions, spanning a period of decades!

Can it be done? There's no question about it: it *has been* done by the inner-city archdiocesan schools of New York. The demographics of the roughly 100,000 students who attend those schools are similar to those for New York City's million or so public schools students: 89 percent are minorities; 93 percent are from families below the poverty line; 60 percent come from single-parent households. But 99 percent of parochial school students complete high school, and 90 percent go on to college—a far better record than holds among the public schools. Moreover, the cost of educating a child in an inner-city parochial school is about half that of educating a child in the public school system.

The basic difference lies in the imposition of standards—academic and disciplinary. If you impose standards, children will meet them. More than that—they *want* standards. Those who have been in charge of the public school system over the years, have failed to grasp that fundamental notion. Indeed, many have concluded and have operated on the assumption that minority children are incapable of achieving academic and disciplinary standards! That is wrong and highly *discriminatory*.

Will it be easy to do what I'm suggesting? Not by a long shot! The hue and cry of the vested interests will be deafening. A campaign will be mounted the likes of which has never been seen in the history of the state. Legislators will be besieged with promises of support and threats of opposition. It will take the hard work, tenacity, courage, and devotion of many informed and powerful people in and out of government. But it's a fight that must be fought! I can think of no greater cause. The survival of the City of New York hangs in the balance.

Of course, there are a number of excellent schools in the system—but they are rare indeed, and the vast majority of them have been and remain disasters. No right-thinking parent with the wherewithal would think of sending a child to such a school! The trouble is that the wherewithal is far beyond the reach of most parents, and the only other choice is to leave New York City.

When I think of the hundreds of thousands of city kids who wanted an education and didn't get one because of the failure of the system, I could cry!

9

Odd Jobs

In the latter part of December 1994, Governor-elect George Pa-taki asked me to assume the job of director of the Governor's Office of Employee Relations (commonly known as GOER). He was primarily interested in my negotiating collective bargaining agreements between the state and the various unions that represent the State's 191,000 person workforce. I told him that I wasn't in a position to do so.

Shortly thereafter, I received a call from my friend Senator Al D'Amato, who urged me to take the job for a brief period and make an effort to procure the contracts during that limited time frame. It had taken Governor Cuomo's administration two years to procure the collective bargaining agreements that were then in effect but would expire on April 1, 1995. I said to Al that the prospects of my procuring collective bargaining agreements during such a short stint were nil. As always, he was enormously persistent. Finally I agreed to take the job as *acting* director of GOER for a *ninety-day period* and stated that I would serve *without pay*. I thought that by doing it in that way, I would have a certain amount of independence from the administration and a better chance of procuring contracts with the unions. I had the hope that I could gain the confidence of most of the unions because of my background and my experience in dealing with union leaders, and that in the end they would prefer to deal with me rather than someone else.

I learned that the three key people in the GOER office were Al DeMarco, the chief negotiator; Jerry Dudack, the executive director; and Walter Pellegrini, the general counsel. Dudack, who was revered by the staff, had already put in his papers for retirement, and it was expected that Pellegrini was about to be fired.

I met with Brad Race, the secretary to the governor, and Mike Finnegan, the general counsel to the governor, to get a briefing as to what the administration expected. They told me that Governor Cuomo had left a five-billion-dollar deficit and that there would be very little money available for labor contracts. They also told me the governor was very much interested in procuring "contracting out" language in the collective bargaining agreements, whereby the government would be in a position to contract out to the private sector work normally and usually performed by union members. Lastly, they informed me that Walter Pellegrini was indeed going to be let go.

I told them I would do everything in my power to deal with the first two problems, namely, the lack of money and the procurement of "contracting out" language, but that it was essential that Pellegrini remain; they agreed.

I explained the situation at a meeting of my senior staff members during which I also let it be known that I had saved Pellegrini's job. After the meeting was over, Jerry Dudack told me that he had changed his mind about retiring and that he intended to stay on for the period of time during which I would be serving as acting director. I was pleased and moved; that action on his part, plus the saving of Pellegrini's job, gave an instant and much needed boost to morale in the office.

Meetings with the leadership of all of the unions followed, during which we outlined the financial situation of the state and invited them to look at the state's books in order to satisfy themselves as to the state's severe fiscal circumstances. We also underscored the need to have "contracting out" provisions.

We then fashioned a very *realistic* proposed collective bargaining agreement and launched *ongoing* negotiations with *all* unions. I told the leadership of all the unions that I did not have time for the usual dance that frequently takes place in labor negotiations, whereby both sides commence with absurd demands and go from there. I told them that our demands were realistic and that I expected theirs to be the same.

It was apparent from the outset that the best strategy would be to procure an agreement with the Civil Service Employees' Association (CSEA) first and then get the other unions to follow, emphasizing that *no one* would get better terms than CSEA *no matter what*. We chose the CSEA not only because it represented the largest number of state workers but because it was headed by

Danny Donohue, who struck me as a strong labor leader with the capability of dealing in a very practical way with realistic facts and with the ability to sell what would normally be a totally inadequate settlement to his membership.

Al DeMarco negotiated on a daily basis with Ross Hanna, the chief negotiator for Danny Donohue, and while I monitored those negotiations closely, I did not participate. There comes a point in almost every negotiation when the *principals* have to intervene in order to close the deal. I had said to Al, "Let me know when you've gotten to the end and you think it's time for Danny and me to finish." Finally Al came to me and said, "We're there." I met with the governor and Brad Race, brought them up to date, and advised them as to what we hoped to get in the final package. They were pleased with the progress we had made, and they gave what I regarded as tacit approval as to where they wanted to finish.

Al and I and Ross Hanna and Danny Donohue met for drinks in a bar outside of Albany. After some additional progress, Danny and I broke away from Al and Ross, and we struck a deal. Danny, of course, had to get the approval of his negotiating committee, and it was crucial that we maintain secrecy until that approval was forthcoming. Shortly thereafter, Danny brought together the members of his negotiating committee at a hotel outside of Albany, and Al DeMarco and I waited in the wings. It was a long night, there was a lot of back and forth, and more changes were made. Finally, at 3:30 A.M., Danny's negotiating committee approved the package. I called Brad Race at home and explained the terms of the final agreement, which he approved. Thereafter, Danny and I entered into a written memorandum of understanding as to what the new contract would provide.

Danny's membership subsequently approved the terms of the memorandum of understanding, and we had a deal within my ninety-day time frame. It was a four-year contract, which meant that the governor would not have to negotiate a *new* contract until *after* his 1998 reelection campaign. The contract provided for no increase in the first year, no increase in the second year, a 3.5 percent increased in the third year, and an additional 3.5 percent increase in the fourth year. There was a $550 bonus increase and a $700 bonus increase, neither of which went into the pay base and both of which went into effect at times intended to assist the reelection efforts of union leaders. The contract also provided for "contracting out" as per the governor's request. The "contracting out" provisions, however, included substantial protection for those employees whom would be adversely effected. The contract afforded the union an opportunity to participate in the bidding process with respect to work contracted out. It afforded adversely affected employees with preferential hiring with the succeeding entity. It also gave preferential treatment for adversely affected employees under the civil service law and made available education credits in the State University of New York system for those who wanted to retrain and go into other fields. In short, it was a fair and equitable contract, given all of the attendant circumstances, particularly the $5 billion deficit under which the state was laboring. The governor was happy, the union leadership was happy, the union membership was happy, and I was happy and indeed proud that we were able to accomplish what we did within such a short time frame.

When the deal was announced, almost all the other unions signed on immediately, as we thought would be the case with minor variations, of course, to suit specific and peculiar needs of each union. But in substance, the contracts were all the same. It was a significant accomplishment for the governor very early in his first term, and it stood in sharp contrast to the fact that it had taken the Cuomo administration two years to negotiate the previous contract. I returned to Robinson, Silverman, and Jerry Dudack retired.

LONG ISLAND POWER AUTHORITY

Several months later, in the summer of 1995, I received a call from Brad Race telling me that Governor Pataki wanted me to serve on the board of the Long Island Power Authority (LIPA). At that time, Long Island had the highest electric rates in the United States (with the sole exception of the island of Maui in Hawaii). The rates were strangling Long Island's industrial capacity and had become a serious political problem for the governor, although the situation was the result of the Cuomo administration's disastrous arrangement with the Long Island Lighting Company (LILCO) relative to LILCO's nuclear power plant at Shoreham.

I had come to admire Governor Pataki, and I told Brad Race I would be happy to serve on the board of LIPA. Brad called back several days later with a shocker: the governor wanted me to serve as *chairman,* a completely different matter from simply serving on the board. I strongly urged Brad to find someone else who was more knowledgeable about the electrical power industry.

A couple of days later, Brad called back to say that the governor had confidence in my ability to get up to speed and still wanted me to serve as chairman. I told him that I would think about it over the weekend. On Sunday night, the phone rang, and my wife, Jackie, said, "The governor's on the phone."

The governor talked passionately about the importance of LIPA vis-à-vis the economy of Long Island and the state. He talked about the need to reduce electric rates dramatically and foster competition in the delivery of electricity on Long Island. He pledged his total support if I took the job.

He was overpowering, and finally I agreed to serve for three months but no more. "I'll put a crackerjack team in the field; I'll give you a plan with all of the ingredients you want—and then I'm gone!"

He said, "Done," and wished me luck. After we rang off, Jackie said to me, "What have you done now?"

I responded: "Goddamned if I know. But it's very important!"

My first act as chairman of LIPA was to call Lou Tomson, who was the governor's deputy secretary in charge of all state authorities. He was my contact person on the "second floor" of the Capitol in Albany, where the governor's executive offices are located. (Lou Tomson is now the president and CEO of the Lower Manhattan Development Corporation, which was established by Governor Pataki to redevelop the property in and around Ground Zero.) I said, "Lou, I don't know the first thing about electricity. I need a very basic and fundamental course." He said, "I've got just the person for you. One of my assistants is a woman by the name of Anastasia Song. She will sit with you and bring you up to speed."

Anastasia is commonly referred to as Ace, and for good reason.

She is the best! I sat with her for an entire day, during which she took me through the generation of electricity, transmission, distribution, governmental regulation, "stranded costs," and a host of other subjects. She then turned to the situation on Long Island, and it was a total disaster. The biggest problem by far was the Shoreham nuclear plant. It had been trouble from the beginning. LILCO had made mistake after mistake during the course of its construction, and governmental authorities required ever-increasing safeguards. As a result, the community had become deeply concerned. Cost overruns were enormous. But finally it came together, and in the end the Shoreham plant was state-of-the-art. Governmental regulators were satisfied that it was as safe as a nuclear power plant could be. But the community was still worried, particularly those who lived in Suffolk County, which is on the easternmost end of Long Island.

As it turned out, the Shoreham plant never went on line. Just before it was to commence operation, Governor Cuomo entered into a deal with LILCO under the terms of which the plant would be shut down and dismantled, and LILCO would recover the costs of constructing and dismantling the plant—by way of a series of *enormous* rate increases over a period of years! Many accused Governor Cuomo of being motivated by political interests, in that an election was coming up. The charge was that he was trying to make inroads into the Republican stronghold of Suffolk County, where voters were most concerned about radioactive leaks. Cuomo's deal generated the highest electric rates in the continental United States and seriously damaged Long Island's economy. Most in the industry believe that if the Shoreham plant had gone operational, it would now be producing electricity at highly competitive rates to the benefit of the people of Long Island, and at no risk to anyone.

There were other problems with Shoreham and LILCO that I won't go into, and by the end of my conversation with Anastasia, I realized I was in over my head, that the task of running LIPA would consume me totally and indefinitely, and that I owed it to my law partners to get out. When I conveyed that message to Governor Pataki, he told me that he wanted to meet.

I knew he was going to twist my arm, so I asked my law partner Ed Koch to be with me when we met, so that I would be better positioned to resist. Ed, of course, agreed, and the three of us met in one of the conference rooms at our law firm. Governor Pataki is a very bright man and, more importantly, a very nice man. Accordingly, he is very difficult to resist. Within minutes, I folded, much to the amusement of Ed! I did, however, derive one benefit from that meeting: I asked the governor to give me Anastasia Song as my executive director, and he agreed. That choice proved crucial.

Anastasia had been living and working in Albany, but we needed her in New York City. So I gave her the office next to mine at our law offices in Midtown, and I made arrangements for her to stay at the nearby Yale Club at government rates. If I have any talent, it's the ability to assess the talents and character of other people. It doesn't take me long, and I'm rarely wrong. I knew that Anastasia was pure gold, and I was hell-bent on making her comfortable.

In the early days it was just the two of us, and we worked together on a daily basis. We hired accountants, tax lawyers, bond counsel, investment advisers, engineers, and a public-relations expert. We also worked with the existing staff at LIPA. Eventually we fashioned a plan that satisfied all of the governor's requirements: LIPA would issue tax-exempt bonds for the purchase of LILCO, including LILCO's transmission and distribution facilities and its 18 percent interest in a nuclear power plant on Nine Mile Island. With the transfer of LILCO's assets to government ownership, they would no longer be taxable, and double-digit rate savings would be realized instantly. Transmission and distribution would be operated by a private electric company pursuant to agreement.

The more difficult and more important part in terms of *continuing* rate reductions was the introduction of competition on the generating side. LILCO's generating facilities on Long Island had been seriously neglected, and all efforts to find alternate off-island generating facilities that would provide reasonable electric rates proved fruitless. Moreover, our engineers determined that laying a power line under Long Island Sound was not economically feasible.

Anastasia found a solution to this problem: sell off the five existing LILCO generating bundles to five separate companies, purchase *all* of their electricity at the outset, and gradually reduce the guarantee over a period of time until full competition was realized. LILCO's gas company would be sold to another independent party, and the gas company would compete with the electric generating companies for additional savings! It was *pure genius*. Our engineers reported that Ace's plan was both brilliant and doable. We put out a request for showings of interest to the generating industry, and we were inundated with favorable responses.

Having fulfilled my promise to the governor, I returned to Robinson, Silverman when the plan was adopted by the LIPA board, leaving implementation to my successor.

GROUP HEALTH INCORPORATED

I began serving on the board of directors of Group Health Incorporated (GHI) in the mid-1980s and have been its chairman since

Announcing our LIPA plan at Adelphi University on December 7, 1995. From left: Tom Gullotta, Governor Pataki, Dean Skelos, and myself.

June 1990. Thanks to the extraordinary leadership of longtime president and CEO Frank Branchini, it has been a sheer delight.

GHI is a nonprofit corporation that provides medical coverage for about two and a half million New Yorkers, mostly union members, city, state, and federal government employees, and employees of small and middle-sized corporations. GHI provides excellent coverage effectively and efficiently, at highly competitive rates.

One of the programs of which I am particularly proud is our Child Care Plus plan, which provides medical coverage for more than three thousand previously uninsured children in the South Bronx, at incredibly low rates that are subsidized by the state. The program is run in conjunction with St. Barnabas Hospital. I believe that this kind of program should be expanded to cover *all* uninsured children in New York State. It can be done at relatively little cost because the cost of insuring *children* for medical benefits is substantially lower than the cost of insuring older people. Also, I believe there should and can be coverage for *all* families in New York who are ineligible for Medicaid but financially *unable* to pay market rates for realistic medical coverage. In the last analysis, the state winds up paying for such coverage anyway.

As to another GHI program of which I am particularly proud: In 1992, GHI entered into an arrangement with the Board of Education of the City of New York whereby GHI provides teachers to teach special courses at Martin Luther King Jr. High School that prepare students for employment at GHI. Any and all students who pass those courses (as well as those provided in the regular curriculum) are *guaranteed* employment at GHI upon graduation. It's a "win-win-win" for the school, the student, and GHI! I think other corporations ought to enter into similar arrangements.

JUDICIAL SCREENING PANEL

In 1997, Governor Pataki asked me to chair his judicial screening panel for the Appellate Division, First Department. I readily agreed. I can think of no greater responsibility for an elected executive than the appointment of judges. Elected officials come and go, but the judges they appoint go on and on and affect our lives in mind-boggling ways.

The Appellate Division is New York State's intermediate appellate court (the only higher court being the New York State Court of Appeals) and is divided into four departments. The First Department covers Manhattan and the Bronx and is particularly important because Manhattan is the commercial and financial center of the world. To be eligible for the Appellate Division, a judge must have already been elected to the New York State Supreme Court, a lower court of original jurisdiction without limitations.

Under Governor Pataki's initial executive order, in order for an elected Supreme Court judge to be appointed to a particular department, he or she had to be currently sitting within that department. I and others urged the governor to amend his order to allow *any* elected Supreme Court judge in the state to be eligible for *any* department. The governor followed our recommendation, and consequently the number of eligible candidates for each department increased. In my opinion, all departments have been enhanced as a result.

3

INTERESTING PEOPLE
AND EVENTS

10

"Senator Lynch" and the Friendly Sons of St. Patrick

My uncle Tom introduced me to the Friendly Sons dinner some forty years ago, and I haven't missed one since. The dinner is renowned for the tremendous caliber of the speakers it has featured down through the years. The speech begins after dinner, by which time those in attendance are not interested in a lecture but want rather to be entertained! In 1977, Senator Daniel Patrick Moynihan disregarded that fact and launched into a long and serious dissertation. It was a disaster. Soon rumbling and muttering began in the audience, and the noise increased steadily in volume until it became a din. The popping of champagne corks and the clatter of dishes indicated that the audience had gone back to eating and drinking. Then came the cat calls. Moynihan finally responded by challenging his hecklers to meet him in back of the hotel!

In the late fall of 1984, I was having dinner with my old friend Mike Armstrong, who had served as counsel to the Knapp Commission and was also Senator Al D'Amato's lawyer and friend. Mike told me that Senator D'Amato had been asked to speak at the annual dinner of the Friendly Sons of St. Patrick, which takes place on St. Patrick's Day at the Sheraton New York Hotel and Towers. It is a formal affair, attended by approximately three thousand men, mostly Irish. Many of New York's most prominent citizens are present, including the cardinal-archbishop of New York.

Al D'Amato was understandably frightened by the prospect of speaking at the Friendly Sons dinner. So I said to Mike, "Tell Al to be light and short—you can never bomb short." Then I offered an idea for Al's speech. In 1972, William Hughes Mulligan delivered the most famous and best-remembered speech ever delivered at a Friendly Sons dinner. Mulligan's thesis was that Christopher

Columbus was not an Italian navigator but rather an Irishman by the name of Lynch! So I suggested that Al refute Mulligan and reconstitute Columbus as an Italian.

"That's a sensational idea," said Mike. "You've got to write the speech."

"No way," said I, "that's an enormous job and I'm not going to do it."

The next morning, my secretary Sheila told me Senator D'Amato was on the phone. I took the call, and from the other end came: "Jimmy Baby—I understand that you're going to write my speech for the Friendly Sons!" I hardly knew the guy, and already I was "Jimmy Baby"! I said, "No, senator, it's a huge undertaking and you've got writers on your staff to do that for you."

He persisted as only he can—until finally I agreed to do it, on three conditions: (1) he couldn't change a word I wrote; (2) we would rehearse together on St. Patrick's Day until I was fully satisfied that his timing and delivery were on target; and (3) he could not take a drink until after the speech.

He agreed, and I wrote the speech. On St. Patrick's Day, we went over the speech as planned—again and again and again, until he had it down to perfection. That night, his delivery was magnificent. Here's part of it:

> The first time I attended a Friendly Sons dinner was on March 17, 1972. It was on that occasion that your esteemed president, Judge William Hughes Mulligan, made the startling revelation that Christopher Columbus was not an Italian but, rather, an Irishman by the name of Lynch.
>
> Many of you will recall that the most convincing and compelling evidence offered by Judge Mulligan that night was an excerpt from the ship's log of the *Nina,* which described Columbus as having red hair, a light complexion, and blue eyes.
>
> Needless to say, I was devastated by Judge Mulligan's persuasive presentation.
>
> When I went home that night, I said to my mother, "Mama! I've got very bad news. It turns out that our greatest Italian hero, Christopher Columbus, was not an Italian but, rather, an Irishman by the name of Lynch."
>
> Mama let out a shriek and slumped in her chair—and with great anguish in her voice, she said: "Alfonso, that he wasn't an Italian is

bad enough. But an Irishman—that's a dagger in your mother's heart."

Suddenly she became angry. "Alfonso, who tell you this?"

"Mama, it was William Hughes Mulligan, a former professor and dean of the Fordham University School of Law and a distinguished judge of the United States Court of Appeals for the Second Circuit."

To which she responded: "*Va faneballa* Mulligan."

She made me promise that I would devote myself unreservedly to an intense study into the ethnic roots of Columbus with a view towards refuting Mulligan and reconstituting Columbus as an Italian.

I've completed that study, and I'm grateful for the opportunity to lay my proofs before this fair and impartial body.

As you know, Columbus set sail from Palos, Spain, on August 3, 1492. His object was to find a short sea route to the East Indies. It was estimated that the voyage would span twenty-four hundred miles and take a minimum of six months.

During the course of my research, I came across a complete list of all the provisions stowed aboard the *Nina,* the *Pinta,* and the *Santa Maria* prior to embarkation. A careful study of the list shows that not a drop of alcohol was stowed aboard any of the three vessels.

Gentlemen, I ask you, how many Irishmen do you know who would embark upon a six-month voyage without an ounce of whiskey or a single bottle of Guinness Stout?

On the other hand, the list did include thirty-five cans of Progresso tomato paste and twelve cartons of Ronzoni macaroni.

We've all seen the traditional picture of Columbus landing at San Salvador in the Bahamas on October 12, 1492. In that picture, Columbus is holding the flag of Spain in his left hand and a sword in his right, with the point of the sword stuck in the ground. Numerous historians contend that on that occasion Columbus inserted his sword in the ground and stated, "I claim this land in the name of King Ferdinand and Queen Isabella."

Authenticated documents currently in the possession of the Bahamian government indicate that no such words were ever spoken. The Bahamian papers show that when Columbus inserted his sword in the ground, his only words were: "I want the boccie court right here."

Al received a standing ovation. What is more, he received public praise from William Hughes Mulligan, who was the master of ceremonies for the evening.

What I didn't know then was that Al's speech was to mark the beginning of an extraordinarily close friendship that endures to this day. Ever since that night, Al has joked with me by referring to himself as Senator Lynch.[1]

In 1992, Al ran for re-election against Robert Abrams, who was then attorney general of New York State. On election day, Al called and invited me and Ed Koch to dinner. Arthur Finkelstein, Al's media guru, joined us, and throughout the meal Arthur was in constant communication with his office as to exit polls. When Bill Clinton took an early eighteen-point lead over President George H. W. Bush, things seemed bleak for Al, and Arthur was the only one at the table who thought Al still had a shot.

As the night wore on, Al became more and more convinced that he was going to lose and became more and more emotional. But even while Bush was getting clobbered, Arthur Finkelstein insisted that Al was still neck-and-neck with Abrams.

Most people don't know that Al D'Amato, for all of his exterior bravado, is a very caring, sensitive, and emotional man. He started worrying aloud about having let down his mother, his father, and his uncle Alfonso. He talked about the impact his loss would have on his kids, and what would happen to his staff members. He was thinking about everyone except himself.

Then he started to drink. Finally I said to him: "Al, win or lose, you're going to be in front of the media tonight, so stop drinking," and he did. When it came time to go to the campaign headquarters at the Hilton Hotel, Al was convinced he had lost. He turned to Koch and, with tears in his eyes, said: "Ed, please take care of Mama."

It was a very long night, but in the end Al pulled it out! It was one of the happiest events I've ever experienced, almost a miracle.

Al is the best instinctive politician I've ever met, but the re-election campaign he and Arthur Finkelstein ran six years later in 1998 was a real letdown. Al isn't very pretty, and he made some impish—but nonetheless incredibly stupid—gaffes (such as sing-

---

[1] I gave some assistance to Governor Pataki and Mayor Giuliani when they addressed the Friendly Sons in 1996 and 2000, respectively They were both terrific.

ing "Old MacDonald Had a Farm" on the floor of the Senate; imitating Judge Lance Ito on the "Imus" radio show; and calling his opponent Charles Schumer a "putz head"). But over his eighteen years in the Senate, Al delivered for New York like no other senator in the history of the state—roads, bridges, airports, public housing, railroad cars, subway cars, buses, government contracts, jobs galore, Israel, the Swiss banks, crime, the environment, Wall Street, health care, the federal judiciary, women and minorities, and on and on. Moreover, by virtue of his seniority in the Senate, he was poised to do even *more* going forward.

The thrust of Al's 1998 campaign was that his Democratic opponent, Charles Schumer, was an "off-the-wall liberal." While this kind of attack politics had worked against Abrams in 1992, it was old and tired and didn't have a chance six years later against Schumer. Ed Koch and I begged Al and Arthur again and again to get off the liberal theme and to focus on Al's enormous clout and his incredible achievements on behalf of New York—but to no avail.

But you know, things usually work out for the best. Today, Al D'Amato is a very happy man—happier than he's ever been. He's making money for the first time in his life; and he's playing a lot of golf and having a lot of fun! He is making up for the enormous pain and suffering to which he was subjected during his efforts to serve New York State honestly and well.

It's my considered judgment that history will eventually treat Al D'Amato as New York's greatest senatorial producer. In the meantime, New York has already suffered and will continue to suffer immeasurably because he's no longer there.

In 1992, I addressed the Friendly Sons, and let me assure you, I was no less frightened than Al D'Amato had been in 1985. But it worked out well. As a matter of fact, I think it's my best speech. Excerpts can be found in appendix C.

11

Hizzoner: Ed Koch

A GREAT DEAL has been written about the life and times of Edward I. Koch—about his career as a district leader in Greenwich Village, his days as a New York City Councilman, his service as congressman and three-term mayor of New York City. Much of that has been chronicled by Ed himself, in no less than nine books, so there is no need for me to get into any of that, as magnificent as his career has been.

But I want to discuss the Ed Koch I've come to know over the past dozen years, during which time he has been my law partner and he and I have become very close friends.

After his defeat at the hands of David Dinkins in the 1989 Democratic mayoral primary, Ed started thinking about where he was going to go and what he was going to do after leaving the mayoralty. As always, he turned to our mutual friend Allen Schwartz. While a number of large firms had expressed interest in hiring Ed, Allen advised Ed to talk to me about coming to our law firm. Our discussions are described in detail in Ed's most recent book, *I'm Not Done Yet*, and I won't repeat them here. Suffice it to say that he joined Robinson, Silverman on January 1, 1990, and has been with our firm ever since.

The Association of the Bar of the City of New York conducts a roast of a public figure every January. The event, called the Twelfth Night, begins with a play performed by lawyers, during which the guest of honor is "panned." Thereafter, the subject is afforded an opportunity to respond through a designated "defender," who, by tradition, lampoons the public figure even more. In January 1990, I was Ed's designated "defender" at the Twelfth Night, and here are excerpts from my remarks on that occasion:

> My job tonight is to defend Ed Koch. It's my understanding, however, that my defense of Ed is supposed to be much like the defense

that Johnny Addy interposed on behalf of Gladys Gooding many years ago at Madison Square Garden, when it was located at Fiftieth Street and Eighth Avenue. At that time, Johnny Addy was the ring announcer at Madison Square Garden, and on that occasion he entered the ring to announce the main event. He rang the bell several times for attention, and a hush fell over the Garden. Addy then announced, "Gladys Gooding will now sing and play the National Anthem." At that point, a drunk in the balcony got up and shouted out at the top of his lungs, "Gladys Gooding is a no good goddamn whore." To which Johnny Addy responded, "Nonetheless."

Well, I have no intention of interposing a Johnny Addy defense on behalf of Ed. Ed is my friend and partner, and I intend to defend him to the hilt.

Many of the charges leveled against Ed have been *grossly* exaggerated and *enormously* overblown.

Take, for instance, the allegation that Ed has been intemperate and overly self-indulgent in his attacks upon persons with whom he disagrees, or whom he dislikes.

Now I know that Ed referred to Leona Helmsley as "the Wicked Witch of the West" and "the Queen of Mean." [*Pause*]

And there's no denying the fact that he called Jimmy Breslin a "bumble brain" and a "jerk." [*Pause*]

And I'm aware that he called Jerry Ford an "empty suit." [*Pause*]

And yes, it's widely known that he called Jesse Jackson an "anti-Semite"; Imelda Marcos a "crook"; and no one need remind me that he called Kurt Waldheim a "Nazi pig" and Ronald Lauder a "clown." [*Pause*]

And I'll admit that he called Gary Hart a "turkey" and Donald Trump a "hot dog." [*Pause*]

And obviously I will concede that he called Jack Newfield a "hump," Dan Quayle a "numb nut," and Nancy Reagan a "Barbie doll." [*Pause*]

Nonetheless, that's about it! [*Pause*]

I mean, what's the big deal here? [*Pause*]

Moreover, I would point out that during all of his years in public office Ed never said a single unkind word about Mother Teresa—despite the fact that she was constantly on his nerves. [*Pause*]

Another scurrilous charge leveled against Ed is that after becoming mayor, he sold out his liberal principles and became an archconservative. His enemies have seized upon a handful of moderate suggestions and recommendations that Ed made during his mayoralty—in a ridiculous and absurd effort to portray Ed as a right-wing reactionary.

For example, they point to the fact that shortly after Ed became mayor, he called for the return of public flogging.

And, of course, they make reference to the fact that Ed favors not only the death penalty but a return of the firing squad.

And they make great to-do over Ed's recommendation that wolves be permitted to roam the MTA train yards as an anti-graffiti measure.

And, yes, they've pounced upon Ed's advocacy of the simultaneous invasions of Cuba, Nicaragua, and the Canadian Province of Quebec.

And more recently they've alluded to Ed's position that Noriega be tortured and hung in public—without benefit of a trial.

On the basis of these perfectly reasonable "middle of the road" proposals, Ed's enemies have labeled him a conservative! It's infuriating and makes my blood boil!

Our offices are close together, and we always talk when we arrive at work in the morning. One Monday morning about three weeks after Ed joined the firm, I said to him: "How was your weekend?"

He said, "Well, it was fine, but you know, it's different now. When I was at Gracie Mansion [the mayor's official residence], I had people who took care of all of my needs, and now I have to take care of those needs myself." He had recently moved into an apartment in Greenwich Village, and he told me that on Saturday morning as he was walking down West Ninth Street to buy some provisions at Balducci's on Sixth Avenue, people kept stopping him and saying: "Oh, Mayor, we miss you. You've got to run again." They all received what has since become his standard answer: "No, the people threw me out, and now the people must be punished." As he was approaching Balducci's, a scruffy character on a bicycle saw him coming and hollered: "Hey, Koch, you were a terrible mayor." To which Ed responded, "Fuck you."

After Ed finished telling me this story, he added: "You have no idea how good that made me feel—after having to put up with that kind of bullshit for twelve years!" It's my favorite Koch story and goes to the heart of the joy and relief he has experienced since leaving the mayoralty!

Ed also had a ten-minute radio show that aired on WNEW every weekday morning at 7:40 A.M. He would tape the show early in the morning in his apartment, and we would meet in his office later, when the show aired, and listen to it together. Whenever he said anything even *remotely* critical about Governor Mario Cuomo, the governor would call Ed and lecture him, at considerable length, as to why the criticism was unwarranted. So whenever Mary Garrigan, Ed's longtime executive assistant, would poke her head into his office right after the show aired, we knew exactly what she was going to say: "Mr. Mayor, the governor's on the line." It was like clockwork. Talk about "rabbit ears!"

Ed Koch is multifaceted. He is highly emotional and quick to cry, particularly in cases where an elderly person or a young person has been done an injustice or a hurt. He is exceptionally bright and has the memory of an elephant, particularly with respect to people who have crossed him. And he very rarely forgives. Time and again, people who have "betrayed" him (his term) will come to him seeking his support, and almost invariably they will be reminded of their transgression and rejected.

Ed *adored* his mother. He loved his father, admired and respected him despite his failings and foibles. And he loved and looked up to his older brother, Harold, who was big, raw-boned, tough, and an outstanding athlete. Ed delights in telling an apocryphal story about how his mother used to say, "Harold, you go out and play baseball. Ed, you sit in the corner and study to be mayor." The apple of Ed's eye is his sister, Pat. I think he sees in her a reflection of his beloved mother. Ed is a very supportive and caring uncle and he is beloved by all of his nephews and nieces and grandnephews and grandnieces.

Ed knows *nothing* about sports. He won't know second base from a hockey puck. While he was mayor, whenever he went to a baseball game at Shea Stadium or Yankee Stadium, he would bring Allen Schwartz and Allen's son David, both of whom are baseball aficionados. One time, a reporter who was aware of Ed's ignorance of baseball tried to embarrass him with questions such as, "What's the infield fly rule?" After each question, Ed simply turned to David and said, "Tell him, David," and David supplied the correct answers. Finally the frustrated reporter blurted out:

"Don't you know *anything?*" To which Ed responded: "I know this kid's name is David."

Ed values his reputation as his most treasured possession. His concern about preserving his good name is best illustrated by what he went through during his third term as mayor.

During that term, Donald Manes, the borough president of Queens, and Harold Friedman, the chairman of the Democratic Party of the Bronx, were charged with serious misconduct, and major scandals followed. Although Ed had nothing to do with their improprieties, and despite the fact that neither was part of his administration, Ed was haunted by the prospect that they would implicate him in an effort to extricate themselves, and that his reputation would be destroyed. He was also cognizant of the fact that under federal law, an indictment may be procured on the basis of accomplice testimony only, without corroboration. Finally he was concerned that Rudy Giuliani, who was the U.S. attorney for the Southern District of New York at the time, would squeeze Friedman and/or Manes so tightly that they would implicate Ed, although there was no basis for doing so. (Giuliani never did.) The situation became so intense that Ed couldn't sleep at night and didn't want to get out of bed in the morning. Finally he *seriously* contemplated the prospect of committing suicide. During those darkest hours he received counsel, advice, consolation, and reassurance from his dear friend John Cardinal O'Connor, and he weathered the storm.

There was another Catholic clergyman who provided Ed with comfort during those black days. Ed went to the South Bronx by helicopter to attend the Special Olympics for Disabled Children, which was sponsored by the New York Archdiocese. When he alighted the helicopter, he was approached by his friend, Monsignor John J. Kowsky, the chaplain of the NYPD.

"Mayor," said Kowsky, "May I be frank with you?"

(*Oh, my God,* thought Koch, *here it comes—the worst is on the way.*) "Of course," replied Koch.

"No," said the monsignor, "can I really be candid?" By this time, Koch had himself indicted, convicted, and in jail.

"Yes, Monsignor," said Ed, "what is it?"

At that point, Kowsky looked around cautiously and said, "Fuck 'em all." It was an act of great faith and loyalty. Ed was overwhelmed and deeply grateful. It was also like getting a reprieve from the governor!

But perhaps the fear that most doggedly haunts Ed is the fear of becoming irrelevant, of no longer being a "player." He fights against it on a daily basis, and his efforts have succeeded. In recent years, he has written columns for *The New York Post,* the *Daily News,* and *Newsday.* He has taught at New York University. He lectures across the country and is interviewed by the media on almost a daily basis with respect to current events. He reviews movies and critiques restaurants. He does a twice-weekly radio dialogue with Al D'Amato for Bloomberg Radio, and they collaborate on a regular *New York* magazine column called "I'm Right and You're Wrong," in which they debate the political issues of the day. They also do a weekly half-hour show together on New York 1, a local TV station. Their success is due to their extraordinary personalities and their strong personal relationship. From what I have seen, Ed Koch will never retire and will be relevant until the day he dies—and for several days thereafter.

I edit all of Ed's editorial pieces. Don't get me wrong—they are written by *him,* and on substance it's *all* Koch—but every once in a while I get to make a point, and the process is great fun for both of us. Each time we finish a piece, Ed smiles broadly and proclaims: "It's our best!" I also serve as Ed's personal lawyer.

Ed is overweight and struggles mightily to keep his weight down. But he loves to eat, and there is no form of food that he doesn't savor. Ed has been on every diet known to humankind, and while he makes progress from time to time, he inevitably has a relapse. On the other hand, he goes to the gym every morning without fail and takes more pills on a daily basis than are distributed by St. Vincent's Hospital.

Ed consumes *all* of New York City's newspapers every day. They are his daily nourishment. He is the most informed person I know. But he has written almost as many books as he's read! When he gives a speech, he *never* reads from a prepared text. He has an extraordinary sense of humor—uniquely Koch—thanks to God-given instinct, timing and delivery, and incredible facial expressions. Whenever he goes out of town to give a speech, he is *obsessed* with the notion of returning at the *earliest* possible moment!

Ed and I have shared many stories over the years, but only rarely has he mentioned his service in the army during World War II. "I landed in France on D-day plus three," said Ed when the subject first came up. "D-day plus three *months*," he added, and we laughed. But then he told me a poignant story about a comrade named Michael Berrigan, who stepped on a land mine that blew his foot off. Ed saw it happen. "I was horrified," Ed said. He made his way to his friend's side, slowly and carefully, in a state of sheer terror, and stayed with him until the medics arrived. Years later, when Ed was mayor, Michael Berrigan's son visited City Hall to thank Ed for saving his father's life. Unfortunately, Ed was at lunch when the son arrived, but when Ed got the message, he contacted the son immediately and *denied* that he had *saved his father's life.* Many politicians would have reacted differently. Ed literally cannot tell a lie!

He loved Mother Teresa. One time while he was mayor, Ed called her at her office in the Bronx and asked her to come to City Hall to discuss the establishment of a hospice for people with AIDS. Mother Teresa declined, saying she was too busy.

"But, Mother," insisted Ed, "I'll send a car for you."

"No," said Mother Teresa, "I'm just too busy."

"Mother," said Ed, "I'll send a police car with lights and a siren."

"With lights and a siren?" she said. "I'll come!" She later established the hospice in Lower Manhattan.

Ed views his twelve years as mayor as his greatest achievement, and he defends his administration as a tigress defends her cubs. No criticism, from whatever source, goes unanswered. He revels in his accomplishments and is enormously proud of those who served in his administration (almost all of them). He has lunch with former members of his administration regularly, and they have a birthday party for him every year at the Hilton Hotel.

Ed has brought our law firm recognition, good counsel, and sound advice to our partners and clients, and he has enhanced our quality of life immeasurably—especially mine. He hasn't produced business, but we love him all the same. Believe it or not, in *that* regard he's shy!

While not particularly religious, Ed is extremely proud of his Jewish heritage and is always in the forefront of the fight against

Ed Koch and Mother Teresa at City Hall.

anti-Semitism. He has spoken out in defense of Israel, frequently to his own detriment. He will always do so. As he says: "I am a proud Jew."

The relationship between Ed and Cardinal O'Connor was extraordinary and well-known. In 1989, they wrote a book, entitled *His Eminence and Hizzoner,* in which they set forth their differences in amicable fashion. For me, the book stands for the proposition that you can disagree without being disagreeable. Would that we all could respect the deeply held convictions of others without vitriol.

Ed frequently attended Masses said by Cardinal O'Connor at St. Patrick's Cathedral. He would always sit in the front pew, and the cardinal would recognize his presence by saying things like, "We are very pleased that so many non-Catholics are with us this evening, and for those who won't know what to do, I suggest that you watch Mayor Ed Koch and do what he does." Or: "I see that Mayor Koch is in place, so let the Mass begin!" They were like brothers.

Ed Koch is pro-choice, but believes that *at some point* during pregnancy a fetus becomes a person, and he favors a ban on so-called partial-birth abortions. About two years ago, Ed said to me: "Jim, I have substantial differences with the cardinal on a host of subjects, including abortion, and yet we enjoy an extraordinary friendship. But others such as Mario Cuomo and Geraldine Ferraro, whose views are somewhat similar to mine, have been chided publicly by the cardinal." I told him the reason was simple: the cardinal expects much more of Catholics than he does of non-Catholics.

"In the eyes of the Church," I explained, "you are invincibly ignorant. Through no fault of your own, you do not recognize the Holy Roman Catholic Church as the Church of God. Accordingly, if you lead the good life, as you do, you will attain Heaven." Ed was quite pleased with the explanation, and when I shared our conversation with the cardinal, he was hysterical.

Like Ed and the cardinal, Ed and I have our disagreements. In 2000, Ed decided to march with Hillary Clinton in the St. Patrick's Day Parade, and accordingly I decided not to join them, even though Ed and I had marched together in the two previous parades. Hillary was booed in an extraordinary manner, and although Ed is by far the most popular person to march in the parade, his presence failed to overcome the negative reaction she generated! He was very depressed at not having received his usual adulation. When he told me so, my response was, "Shame on you. You deserve to be depressed!"

In 1998, Al D'Amato, who comes from a small village on Long Island called Island Park, marched in the St. Patrick's Day Parade with Ed. After listening to cheers go up for Ed block after block, he finally expressed his amazement.

"Al," said Ed, "you have to understand—this is my Island Park!"

My friendship with Ed Koch is unique. While we agree on most things, we have differences that are deeply held. And yet our friendship not only endures but becomes stronger. That's because it's grounded in mutual respect. Any other kind of friendship isn't worth a whole hell of a lot!

Ed Koch, thrusting his hands aloft and proclaiming, "It's me" during the St. Patrick's Day Parade in 1999. From left to right: Katie Lapp, myself, Ed Koch, Lt. Governor Donohue, Governor Pataki, Bill Plun-kett, and Jim McGuire.

12

His Eminence:
John Cardinal O'Connor

As I've said, I first met His Eminence John Cardinal O'Connor soon after I was appointed to chair what became known as the Gill Commission. The next time I met with him was in 1990, at a dinner party at Ed Koch's apartment, on which occasion he complimented the work of our commission. Thereafter I had breakfast with him at his residence on a number of occasions and later became deeply involved in the lawyers division of the Cardinal's Committee of the Laity, which conducts an annual luncheon at the Grand Hyatt Hotel every September and gives the proceeds to the inner-city archdiocesan schools.

In May of 1992, the cardinal asked me to serve as general counsel to the board of trustees of St. Patrick's Cathedral, which he chaired. (I've represented that board ever since and continue to do so under the leadership of His Eminence Edward Cardinal Egan.) Cardinal O'Connor and I became friends, and there was no better friend than he.

Cardinal O'Connor sat on the altar at my daughter Rose's wedding to Frank Hearn at St. Patrick's Cathedral in August 1995. (If I were to choose a lifelong mate for my beloved Rose, I would have chosen Frank Hearn. He's that good!) He also baptized my grandson, James, in the private chapel at his residence, in June 1999. Upon baptizing James, the cardinal announced: "He's a Kat-lick!"

The cardinal passed away in 2000, and ever since his death I've gone to St. Patrick's regularly to visit his crypt under the main altar, where his remains lie with those of the previous bishops of New York. The first time I did so, I said to him: "Eminence, now you know what a bum I really am, but let's get all of that behind us. After all, my heart's in the right place!"

The cardinal and I got along well from the outset, and there

James's christening. From left: Dennis, Frank Hearn, James, Rose, Patrick, Cardinal O'Connor, my mother-in-law, myself, and Jackie.

were several reasons why. His father was a union member and a union activist, as was mine. I've represented unions for the past thirty-six years, and it's my favorite pastime. The cardinal was intensely pro-union. He deeply believed in and carried out the dictates set forth in the papal encyclicals "Rerum Novarum" and "Quadragesimo Anno." During his tenure as archbishop of New York, he was instrumental in the settlement of numerous labor disputes both publicly and (more often) privately. And he supported union legislative causes consistently.

His differences with some of the unions that represent those employed by the inner-city archdiocesan schools caused him enormous pain and suffering. He was keenly aware that those who served in those schools were underpaid and that the benefits they received were too low. On the other hand, one of his primary religious responsibilities was to keep the schools in existence and within the financial reach of parents who desperately wanted their children to attend those fine institutions. He fully recognized the rights of those employees as working persons, including their right to picket him personally—which they did, at his offices on First Avenue and at his residence behind St. Patrick's Cathedral. But he objected to and would not countenance demonstrations in front of St. Patrick's Cathedral or any other Catholic church during the Holy Sacrifice of the Mass. The Mass is the church's most sacred ritual, during which bread and wine are transformed into the body and blood of Jesus Christ—not symbolically, mind you, but literally—and the cardinal regarded the willful and deliberate desecration of that sacred ritual, by teachers of children in the Catholic school system, as setting an appalling and unacceptable example for their young charges.

Another thing that the cardinal and I had in common was the Marine Corps. The cardinal served as a chaplain in the Navy for twenty-six years, attained the rank of rear admiral, and was appointed as the chief of all chaplains in the military service. He served as chaplain for the Third Marine Division in Vietnam, and he had a very warm spot in his heart for marines.[1]

Several years ago, he told me that he had once been addicted to cigars. He went on to say that while on a helicopter in a combat zone in Vietnam, the pilot deferred to him as the senior officer aboard and sought his direction as to which way to return the helicopter to home base—the long way or the short way. The long way was safer, but the fuel supply was perilously low. The short way was highly dangerous. Admiral O'Connor directed the pilot to proceed directly to home base and into the teeth of hostile fire. He then and there promised God that if God delivered them safely, he would stop smoking cigars. They arrived at home base safely, and he never smoked another cigar.

The cardinal and I were both educated by the Jesuits, I at Holy Cross and he at Georgetown. From time to time, I would remind him that President Clinton was a Georgetown alumnus—but only when he was in the best of moods!

I loved his sense of humor enormously, and he enjoyed mine. We had a lot of human chemistry.

By far the greatest indignity and the deepest hurt Cardinal

---

[1] On June 18, 2002, the cardinal was honored posthumously by the Marine Corps at a sunset parade at the Marine Corps's Iwo Jima Memorial in Washington, D.C. I am proud to say that I arranged that for my dear friend.

O'Connor suffered during his sixteen years as archbishop of New York took place on December 10, 1989, when the members of ACT UP invaded St. Patrick's Cathedral during the Holy Sacrifice of the Mass. The protesters threw the Holy Eucharist on the floor and stepped on it, the equivalent of throwing Christ to the ground and stepping upon Him. Banners were unfurled proclaiming, GET YOUR ROSARIES OFF OF MY OVARIES, and making reference to CARDINAL O'CONDOM. Other banners depicted Christ in homosexual stances. I can recall no conduct, on the part of any organization, more willful and deliberate, more insensitive, more offensive, more brutal, more strident, or more intolerant. In the face of that incredible outrage, Cardinal O'Connor rose to the occasion and urged his congregation to turn the other cheek and pray for those who were engaged in this mind-boggling desecration. I believe that his intervention prevented mayhem.

What ACT UP did is even more distressing when one considers that the Catholic Church has spent more money and done more for AIDS victims than any other institution in New York, including the state itself. And the Church will continue to care for AIDS victims despite the atrocities heaped upon Her, because caring for the sick is one of Her many sacred missions. Cardinal O'Connor regularly extended himself personally to AIDS victims in a most loving fashion, visiting with them in the hospital, talking to them and their family members, encouraging them, feeding them, helping to provide them with medical care, praying for them, and yes, emptying their bedpans.

His Holiness Pope John Paul II visited New York City in the fall of 1995, and His Eminence invited me and a number of others to his residence to meet the Holy Father. It was bigger than having my arm rubbed by baseball pitcher Whitlaw Wyatt when I was a kid! The Holy Father greeted us one by one. Among our group was a Franciscan nun by the name of Sheila Flanagan; next to her was her father, Peter Flanagan. When the Holy Father came to Sheila, his face lit up, he took her by both hands, and he asked her name.

"Sheila, Your Holiness," she replied.

"To what order do you belong?" he asked.

"The Franciscans, Your Holiness."

"Where is your mission?"

"In Nashville, Tennessee, Your Holiness."

"What kind of work do you do there?"

"We shelter, feed, and clothe the poor, Your Holiness."

"Oh, Sheila!" the Holy Father exclaimed. He then embraced her warmly, blessed her and her order, and moved on to the next person, Sheila's father, who was unusually tall. The Holy Father looked up at his face and said, "You look a lot like Sheila."

Everyone in the room broke into laughter. When Mr. Flanagan explained that he was Sheila's father, the Holy Father joined in the laughter.

His Holiness went on to greet the others who were in attendance. Then, as he was taking his leave, he suddenly turned around, pointed to Sheila, and said, "Sheila"—as if he were putting her name, what she is, and what her order does, into his mental computer.

He is the quintessence of love and goodness. When I was a boy growing up in Waterbury, Connecticut, I never dreamed that one day I would meet a pope of the Holy Roman Catholic Church, the vicar of Christ on earth!

Meeting the pope at the cardinal's residence.

The first lawyers division luncheon of the Cardinal's Committee of the Laity was held at the Grand Hyatt Hotel in 1990. The first honoree and recipient of the St. Thomas More Award was William Hughes Mulligan, whom I had the honor of introducing. (Excerpts from my introductory remarks can be found in appendix D.) I approached the task with considerable trepidation. As I stated earlier, Mulligan had been my professor and dean at Fordham Law School; he was my friend; and he was the best public speaker I've ever heard. Unfortunately, Mulligan had suffered a stroke and was unable to respond verbally to my introduction. He stood with tears running down his face as he received a thunderous, standing ovation.

Afterward, the cardinal presented him with the award, and there followed one of the most extraordinary events I have ever witnessed. Mulligan had represented the archdiocese in a reapportionment case in Yonkers, New York, and at one point there was an apparent misunderstanding between Mulligan and the archdiocese as to the Church's position. Consequently, Mulligan was forced to recant a previously announced position, to his grave professional embarrassment, and those of us who knew him were aware that he had been deeply wounded.

After placing the award around Mulligan's neck, the cardinal apologized publicly for having done him an injustice. The cardinal then began to cry uncontrollably, repeating over and over again, "I'm sorry, Bill," in front of seven hundred lawyers and judges. It was stunning. Obviously he had been waiting for an occasion to right what he recognized as a wrong for which he was, at least in part, responsible. Everyone at that luncheon came away with an awesome respect for the cardinal's integrity and sense of justice. Not too long after that, Mulligan died, and Cardinal O'Connor was the principal celebrant and eulogist at his funeral Mass.

The cardinal had a delicious sense of humor and he flashed it regularly. Once, at a lawyers' division luncheon of the Cardinal's Committee of the Laity, I introduced Cardinal O'Connor as "His Eminence John Cardinal *Spellman*." No sooner were the words out of my mouth than I added: "I think I just lost a client." To which the cardinal responded, "James, you didn't just *lose* a client—you *buried* one."

Years ago I introduced my wife, Jackie, to the cardinal by saying, "Your Eminence, this is my wife Jackie." His response: "You mean there are others?"

And on December 15, 1995, at a Mass at St. Patrick's, we were celebrating his fiftieth year as a priest. The cathedral was jammed with dignitaries religious and lay, the cardinal's relatives, and scores of friends and admirers. The homilist was William Cardinal Baum. Towards the end of his remarks, Cardinal Baum said the following about Cardinal O'Connor: "Did you know that his patron saint is St. John Fisher, another bishop and cardinal, who in another age spoke fearlessly in defense of the faith? John Fisher suffered death by beheading because of his steadfastness, and John O'Connor has looked always to his patron saint as an example and intercessor."

In response, Cardinal O'Connor told of his efforts to follow doggedly in the footsteps of his patron saint, but he expressed the hope that his demise would be *somewhat more peaceful and serene* than that of his beloved mentor! The cathedral rocked with laughter.

On January 17, 1993, I was present when Bishop Henry Mansell said his first Mass as a bishop at St. Patrick's Cathedral. Given the occasion, Bishop Mansell sat in Cardinal O'Connor's episcopal chair throughout the celebration. Cardinal O'Connor, of course, was on the altar and at the end of the Mass got up and said: "Don't get too comfortable in that chair, Henry."

On September 11, 1997, the Holocaust Museum at Battery Park City was dedicated. It was a terrible day—rainy, cold, and windy—but the entire New York City Jewish community turned out for the occasion, including the revered Holocaust survivor Elie Wiesel. The moderator of the event was Robert M. Morgenthau, the district attorney of New York County and a prime mover and guiding force in the establishment of the museum, together with Peter Kalikow.

As chairman of the Battery Park City Authority, I was seated in the front row, next to Cardinal O'Connor, who was to deliver the opening benediction. While Morgenthau was introducing His Eminence, I saw the cardinal take out a piece of paper from his pocket and scribble a few notes on it.

The cardinal then delivered one of the most electrifying and impassioned speeches I have ever heard. He began by apologizing to the Jews for the failure of Catholics to do more for the Jews during the Holocaust. Up to that point, no Catholic prelate at his level had ever made such an abject apology. He then went on to talk about the importance of the bond between Jews and Catholics, referring to Jews as his "ancient brothers and sisters" and quoting extensively from the Old Testament.

Several months later, my friend Mel Stein called to tell me that Elie Wiesel and others in the Jewish community wanted a copy of the cardinal's speech. I told Mel that there was no text, just those few notes the cardinal had scribbled on a small piece of paper that morning.

In August 1999, a tumor was discovered on the cardinal's brain, and he underwent extensive surgery. Thereafter he was subjected to intense radiation and finally went on steroids that bloated him grotesquely. His disease was terminal, and he knew it, but he was resolved to do as much as he could for as long as he could. And that's what he did.

The radiation therapy made his hair fall out, and so on one of my visits to his residence, I brought him a gift of a shoulder-length blond wig. He roared with laughter—and then put it on! I said: "Eminence, I think it's kind of cute."

"It won't do," responded the cardinal, "It clashes with the red!" He then removed the wig and said, "Only you, James, only you!"

On January 20, 2000, we had an eightieth birthday party for His Eminence at the Waldorf-Astoria. The party was initiated by B. J. Harrington, the finest Catholic layman I've ever known, and was attended by cardinals, archbishops, and bishops from across America, as well as by heads of religious orders and by governmental officials, politicians, captains of industry, relatives of the cardinal, and many of his close personal friends. The event raised over $5 million for the archdiocese. It was our final testimonial, and the event gave the cardinal an opportunity to be with and talk with his colleagues and friends while he was still able to do so.

Part of the proceeds from that event went to fund a chair the cardinal established at St. Joseph's Seminary in Yonkers, New York, for Jewish studies. Accordingly, all future seminarians who go through St. Joseph's Seminary will be taught the importance of bonding with the members of the Jewish faith.

The dinner was also attended by the papal nuncio, the pope's representative at the dinner. When the papal nuncio spoke, he, of course, brought the warm personal birthday wishes of the Holy Father. The cardinal's remarks were, as usual, laced with delightful humor, a lot of which dealt with the fact that he was at the end of his tenure as archbishop of New York.

This picture was taken immediately following the cardinal's 80th birthday celebration at the Waldorf-Astoria. It was our last picture together.

The relationship between the cardinal and the pope was extraordinary. They loved each other as brothers. I'm told by a most reliable source that they joked with each other in Latin.

The cardinal died on May 3, 2000, at 8:05 P.M. In the days that followed, the news of his death dominated the media in a way which was reminiscent of the assassination of President John F. Kennedy. The cardinal's funeral was held at St. Patrick's Cathedral on Monday, May 8, 2000, and it was a national event. The celebrant of the Mass was the Vatican secretary of state, Angelo Cardinal Sodano, and the homilist was Bernard Cardinal Law, the archbishop of Boston, the cardinal's close and dear friend.

I sat with Al D'Amato, former New York governor Hugh L. Carey, and former mayors Abe Beame, Ed Koch, and David Dinkins. Among the others in attendance were President and Hillary Clinton, Vice President Al Gore and his wife, Tipper, Governor Pataki and his wife, Libby, Mayor Rudy Giuliani, Senators Daniel Moynihan and Charles Schumer of New York, Senators Pete Domenici of New Mexico and Bob Kerrey of Nebraska, and George W. Bush, who was still governor of Texas, and his wife, Laura. Former President George H. W. Bush sat with the cardinal's family, in accordance with instructions that had been left by the cardinal (the two had been very close friends and mutual admirers).

Cardinal O'Connor was many things. He was extraordinarily bright. He was extremely articulate. He wrote magnificently. He was compassionate, caring, and understanding. He had a wonderful sense of humor. He had electrifying leadership qualities. But what I admired most about him was that when it came to faith and morals, *he never flinched—no matter what.*

He was devoted to helping the poor, the homeless, the sick and disabled, the abused and abandoned, young and old; and his opposition to discrimination, the death penalty, and warfare were no less intense than his positions on abortion and euthanasia.

While the cardinal's accomplishments were extraordinary, I believe he will be best remembered for his relentless and dogged efforts in forwarding the pro-life movement in the United States, a task given to him by the Holy Father. Fanatics and zealots on both sides share responsibility for the discord and disharmony that the issue of abortion has generated. On the anti-abortion side, some deranged and terribly misguided people have engaged in the murder of abortionists. Nothing could do more damage to the pro-life cause. In addition, there are those who would use physical force to block a woman from gaining access to an abortionist's office. And there are those who adhere to the mistaken view that a mother must die to preserve the fetus. That has never been Catholic doctrine. (Under the principle of the so-called double effect, a fetus may be taken when a woman is in imminent danger of death and the taking is necessary for and incidental to the primary purpose of saving the life of the woman.)

On the other side, there are those who favor partial-birth abortion, a gruesome surgical procedure that involves sucking the brain from a fetus's cranium so that it collapses and falls out of the womb. Partial-birth abortion is more accurately termed infanticide. The American Medical Association opposes partial-birth abortions and has taken the position that there are *no circumstances* when such a procedure would be necessary to save the life of a mother! In the meantime, the pro-choice media refuses to describe the procedure, and indeed covers it up by using the phrase "late-term abortion." They know that if they describe the procedure, the argument against a ban on partial-birth abortion will be in serious jeopardy. More than that, it will be over!

But there has been progress. Thirty-three states have banned that kind of atrocity. Congress has twice passed a ban on that kind of procedure (on each occasion, President Clinton vetoed the legislation). As more and more Americans become aware of what the procedure involves, and as legislators, please God, become more adept at drafting the appropriate legislation, partial-birth abortions will be banned throughout America, and Cardinal O'Connor's great crusade will be vindicated.

While we deeply grieve the loss of Cardinal O'Connor, we know that the Catholic Church will go on, that Cardinal Egan and others will carry out its mission in their own ways, and that ultimately the Church will prevail.

13

Doris Duke and Her Legacy

JAMES BUCHANAN ("BUCK") DUKE was a self-made man who amassed a fortune in the tobacco and electrical industries and in real estate and other investments. When he died, on October 10, 1925, his daughter, Doris, became the wealthiest woman in the world.

While I never met Doris Duke, I've read a great deal about her and have talked to many people who knew her, and I believe that she regarded her father as the most precious person in her life. While she was still in her teens, she instituted legal action to block her mother her from selling the 2,800-acre estate James Duke had built at Somerville, New Jersey, and which he had loved dearly. And young Doris won!

Her father had warned her to beware of predators in pursuit of her wealth. She married twice, and her first husband was a handsome young man by the name of Johnny Cromwell, from a prestigious social family in Pennsylvania. The Cromwells were not awash with money, and Johnny was apparently ill-suited for earning money on his own. Their honeymoon lasted for one year, during the course of which they went around the world. At one point on the trip, Cromwell allegedly asked Doris what his monthly allowance was going to be. I suspect that that inquiry sowed the seeds of the divorce that followed about five years later. Doris's second marriage, to the international playboy Porfirio Rubirosa, lasted about six months.

Doris was a superb jazz pianist and wrote jazz that was acclaimed. She sang regularly with a black choir in New Jersey and was a devotee and patron of the performing arts, especially dance. She served as a war correspondent in Europe during World War II. She traveled throughout the world and counted numerous heads of state among her friends. She gathered an extraordinary collection of Islamic art. She built an estate called Shangri-La at the foot of Diamond Head in Oahu, Hawaii, overlooking the Pacific Ocean. During World War II, she loaned Shangri-La to the U.S. Navy. Duke Gardens, which she built on the estate in Somerville, New Jersey, ranks among the most beautiful indoor gardens in the world.

She had a legendary love for animals—cats, dogs, horses, cows, chickens, pigs, donkeys, and yes, even camels—and they were all treated like royalty. (One summer she introduced a magnificently festooned brace of camels to Newport society at her estate, which was known as Rough Point.) I think she trusted animals more than she did people, since they come without agendas.

She never bore a child, but she adopted Charlene Gail Hefner, who was commonly known as Chandi. Tragically, they had a bitter falling out, and Doris sought unsuccessfully to disinherit Chandi.

There is no doubt in my mind that Doris Duke was an extraordinarily good person, although she was maligned viciously and frequently by sensationalists in the media. She was direct and forthright in her dealings with people. She despised pretense. She was a perfectionist and, as such, was demanding of herself and other people. Not only did she treat those who worked with her with dignity but she took care of them and their families in a manner that was extraordinary; in return, they loved her and gave her their full devotion. Those who continue to work at the various properties she left behind (Rough Point in Newport, Shangri-La in Hawaii, and the estate in Somerville, New Jersey) continue in their devotion and dedication to her. To this day, if you ask one of them why such and such is this way or that way, the response is always the same: "That's the way Ms. Duke wants it," as if she might still be on the premises.

It is estimated that Doris Duke gave away approximately 30 percent of her wealth during her lifetime. And she gave simply for the sake of doing it, without any expectation of recognition or praise from others. I was amazed to learn, from people who were in her employ, about her many acts of generosity, almost all of which were done without any publicity. I am sure that that quality of and by itself merited her Heaven when she died, in Los Angeles, on October 28, 1993, at the age of eighty.

As soon as Doris Duke's will was submitted for probate, intense and bitter litigation broke out. The principal beneficiary was a man by the name of Bernard Lafferty, who had served as Doris's butler during her final years. Although an alcoholic and a drug addict, Lafferty was a charmer and managed to win Doris's favor towards the end of her life. Most of the litigation centered on Lafferty's activities both before and after Doris's death. The matter was settled only after several years of litigation and millions of dollars in legal fees.

Under the terms of the settlement agreement, a board of trustees was designated for the Doris Duke Charitable Foundation. The board consisted of J. Carter Brown, the director emeritus of the National Gallery of Art;[1] Marion Oates Charles, a friend and Newport, Rhode Island, neighbor of Doris's; Dr. Harry Demopoulos, one of Doris's doctors in her later years; Nan Keohane, the president of Duke University; John Mack, who was then president and chief operating officer of Morgan Stanley Dean Witter and is now the chief executive officer of Credit Suisse First Boston; and myself.

The board elected me chairman, and I continue in that capacity. At the outset, we were handed $900 million for investment. John Mack initially recommended that we put all of it in index funds, and that's what we did. The markets were right, and the fund profited handsomely. (We have since diversified broadly, and the fund continues to do well.) We hired lawyers, accountants, and investment advisors.

Surrogate Judge Eve Preminger, who presided over the settlement, directed us to recommend another trustee, who was to be a doctor. We interviewed a host of distinguished candidates, including Nobel Prize winners and presidents of major hospitals, before finally selecting Dr. Anthony S. Fauci, who was in charge of the infectious-disease section of the National Institutes of Health and was the world's leading authority on AIDS. He became the seventh member of our board, and what a magnificent choice he was. (By the way, he's a Holy Cross man!)

---

[1] J. Carter Brown died on June 19, 2002, leaving behind an enormous record of achievement in the arts.

We then launched a nationwide search for a president of the foundation. In the end, we chose Joan Spero, who had graduated Phi Beta Kappa from the University of Wisconsin; earned a PhD in political science from Columbia University, where she later taught; served as the executive vice president for corporate affairs and communications of American Express; and was lately the undersecretary of state for economic, business, and agricultural affairs under Secretary of State Warren Christopher. She has turned out to be a superb choice.

Early on we decided to have a relatively small staff and to hire consultants for needed expertise.

In 2001, we voted to add John Wilson to the board of trustees. John had enjoyed an incredibly distinguished career at Morgan Stanley and brought to the table extraordinary expertise in the areas of finance and the environment.

Managing a large philanthropy is challenging work but is great fun and enormously satisfying. The foundation has assets of approximately $1.5 billion and distributes more than $50 million a year in grants, in close compliance with the provisions Doris Duke's will. The grant program aims to "make a difference" in the fields of cancer, heart disease, sickle-cell anemia, AIDS, the environment, the performing arts, and the prevention of child abuse. In addition, the foundation has a continuing obligation to maintain Doris's estates in Rhode Island, Hawaii, and New Jersey. Rough Point and Shangri-La have already been opened to the public, as have Duke Gardens.

The Doris Duke Foundation has leveraged its grants to performing-arts organizations by requiring matching endowments and by forging partnerships with other foundations in the City of New York. The foundation contributed $3.5 million to the New Forty-second Street, which houses the Duke on Forty-second Street Theater; and $5 million to Jazz at Lincoln Center and the construction of two state-of-the-art jazz theaters that will be housed at the old Coliseum site on Columbus Circle. And it was a three-and-a-half-million-dollar Doris Duke Foundation grant that was responsible in the main for the restoration of the Brooklyn Academy of Music.

We have utilized the same leveraging devices to secure 32,000 acres of biologically significant landscapes from sprawl in New

Jersey, Rhode Island, and Yellowstone National Park, and along the Gulf Coast. In addition, we have protected over 60,000 acres of critical forest land in the Northern Forest. Our first major grant was one of $5 million that literally saved the Sterling Forest from development. But for that last-minute grant, the governmental grants that were then in place would have lapsed.

Our medical program is devoted to research in the medical areas as set forth in Doris Duke's will. Recent grants have gone to support research in South Africa at the heart of the AIDS pandemic.

I want to end this chapter with an incident that epitomizes Doris in her heyday. At one point, she decided that she wanted to install an ocean-fed saltwater pool at Shangri-La. It is virtually impossible for anyone, under any circumstances, to get permission to draw from ocean waters for such a purpose. But she got it! How did she do it? She also owned a substantial piece of ocean-front property on the other side of Oahu, and she contacted President Franklin D. Roosevelt and told him that if he allowed her

"Shangri-La."

to draw water from the Pacific Ocean for her pool, she would in turn give her other oceanfront property to the people of Oahu. President Roosevelt readily agreed! Incidentally, the pool has a hydraulic diving board that you can raise or lower to the desired level!

14

Hugh L. Carey
Battery Park City

In 1996, several months after my departure from the Long Island Power Authority, I ran into Brad Race and Lou Tomson at Docks, a restaurant on Third Avenue near the governor's New York City executive offices.

"How would you like to be the chairman of the Battery Park City Authority?" asked Brad.

At first I thought he was kidding, but it soon became clear that he was dead serious. I said, "Brad, let me think about it over the weekend, and I'll call you on Monday."

On Sunday night, the phone rang and Jackie picked up. She turned to me and said, "The governor's on the phone." (Apparently the governor does a lot of work from home on Sunday nights.) After some initial pleasantries, he asked me to chair the Battery Park City Authority, and I accepted—I had no trouble with this one. The governor has subsequently reappointed me, and I remain chairman. It's one of the most exciting and rewarding jobs I've ever held.

The first two years proved difficult and enormously time-consuming, primarily because I clashed with John LaMura, who was president and CEO for most of that period. I took control of the day-to-day operations of the Authority during that time. LaMura eventually resigned and was replaced by Timothy S. Carey,[1] who was and remains a godsend!

Battery Park City was renamed Hugh L. Carey Battery Park City several years ago, in honor of the former governor of New York. The renaming was initiated by Governor Pataki.

In the five years prior to the terrorist attack of September 11, 2001, we accomplished a great deal at Battery Park City. We

---

[1] Many ask whether Tim Carey and Hugh Carey are related. They are not.

Opening of Wagner Park, fall 1995. Behind me, from left to right: Governor Pataki, Mayor Giuliani, and Ed Koch. I don't remember what I said, but whatever it was, it appealed to Mayor Giuliani.

opened Rockefeller and Wagner Parks, the Police Memorial, the Holocaust Museum, and the Mercantile Exchange. We built an elementary school and a middle school, six high-rise apartment buildings, a facility for elderly residents, an Embassy Suites Hotel with 463 suites, three new restaurants, and a sixteen-screen cinema. We began construction of a five-star Ritz-Carlton Hotel that would house the Skyscraper Museum, three restaurants, and condominiums overlooking New York Harbor. Construction was also well under way on the Irish Hunger Memorial in honor of the victims of the famine of 1845–50, a facility that would also serve as a international starvation-alert center.

We had broken ground for the world's first "green" (environmentally friendly) high-rise apartment building. Our intention was to demonstrate to the world that such buildings would not only be good for people's health and the environment but would also be economically feasible in the long term. We believed that if we succeeded, the impact on future housing construction would constitute a sea change. On April 11, 2000, former Russian president Mikhail Gorbachev, who now heads Green Cross Interna-

Showing a rendering of the Irish Hunger Memorial to Gerry Adams, president of Sinn Fein, and Governor Pataki.

An evening with President Gorbachev.

tional (an environmental organization), bestowed the Global Green Award on the Battery Park City Authority for our new green building.

And with all of these initiatives, in the years 1996 through 2001 we returned the staggering sum of $380 million in surpluses to the City of New York! We were able to accomplish all of that for a number of reasons: the unstinting encouragement and assistance of Governor Pataki, supportive board members, Tim Carey and his superb staff, and a strong real-estate market.

On the morning of Tuesday, September 11, 2001, I was on my way from my home in Nassau County to Battery Park City with Anthony Robinson, my friend and driver. I read the morning newspapers and then asked Anthony to turn on the radio to news station 1010 WINS. Almost as soon as he did so, we heard a report that an airplane had struck the northern tower of the World Trade Center. Shortly thereafter, a report of a second airplane crashing into the southern tower was announced, and I realized our nation was under a terrorist attack.

Battery Park City is directly across the street from the World Trade Center (they are separated by West Street), and my first thought was for those who live and work in Battery Park City, particularly the children who attend our elementary school, middle school, and Stuyvesant High School. Realizing that I would not be able to get to Battery Park City, I asked Anthony to drive me to our law offices in midtown Manhattan. Upon arrival, I began making telephone calls in an effort to ensure the evacuation of all buildings in Battery Park City. I was relieved to learn that the New York Fire Department, the New York Police Department, and members of our staff had already commenced that process. They managed to evacuate thirty thousand workers from the World Financial Center, as well as seven thousand residents and all of the schoolchildren. (Most were evacuated by ferryboats.) Despite the fact that Battery Park City is directly across the street from the World Trade Center buildings that imploded, not a single fatality or serious injury took place on our premises.

The next day, I tried to get down to Battery Park City, but all my efforts failed. On the morning of Thursday, September 13, I called Brad Race of Governor Pataki's New York City offices and asked him to make state troopers available to drive me to the site, and he did so. After going through checkpoint after checkpoint, we finally made it to Ground Zero.

Our beautiful and beloved Battery Park City had been transformed into a war zone. The scene was littered with debris, including huge chunks of twisted metal from the exteriors of the fallen towers. The entire area was buried under the dust of granulated cement. The American Express Building, the Winter Garden, and the residential complex known as Gateway Plaza were all severely damaged. Crushed fire trucks and other damaged emergency vehicles were all about. It was devastating and at the same time infuriating!

That afternoon, I issued the following press release:

STATEMENT BY JAMES F. GILL
Chairman, Hugh L. Carey Battery Park City Authority
September 13, 2001

As we slowly recover from the horror of the World Trade Center attack, the Battery Park City Authority is profoundly grateful to report that not a single person was killed or injured on Battery Park City's property.

On the other hand, Battery Park City has sustained substantial property damage. The Winter Garden and the American Express Building were struck by falling material. But fortunately neither building sustained any structural damage.

Battery Park City is covered with debris and dust, much of which is granulated concrete, which in some places is three inches deep.

However, I want everyone who lives and works in Battery Park City to know that although we have sustained damage and lives have been disrupted, with the full support and guidance of Governor George E. Pataki, Battery Park City, like the City of New York itself, will shine again. We already have a Web site in operation to help people separated by the disaster to locate each other. The Web address is www.batteryparkcity.org; click on the link to the Locator Board. We are also bringing residents into Battery Park City to rescue pets and get medication etc. Residents should go to Pier 40 at West Houston Street, where they will be escorted into Battery Park City by park enforcement personnel.

We are digging ourselves out. We are engaged in a comprehensive cleanup operation and will repair and rebuild wherever necessary. In this way, we will demonstrate to those who perpetrated these vicious, dastardly, and cowardly attacks that we have prevailed and they have lost.

I was enormously pleased when President Bush announced that not only will those directly involved in the attacks be punished, but all persons and nations who aided and abetted these acts of terror will be punished as well, including those who provided the terrorists with safe harbor.

This was the most depraved and craven attack in the history of the world. It is unmitigated evil, and it must be punished, swiftly and severely.

It is a miracle that our neighborhood escaped death, serious injury, and structural damage, and for this I am deeply grateful to God.

On Friday, September 14, Ed Koch and I joined a number of religious leaders and other dignitaries and were escorted in New York Police Department vans to Ground Zero. We were there to greet President Bush. The image of those courageous rescue workers, sifting through a massive smoking pile of debris by hand in search of survivors, bodies, and body parts, will be forever etched in my memory. No picture can adequately portray the full extent of the destruction and devastation that was wrought by the mindless cowards that inflicted it.

When President Bush arrived on the scene, he immediately began to thank and comfort the police officers and firefighters in the area. At one point, he stood on top of a destroyed fire truck and put his arm around a grimy and exhausted firefighter. The chant "USA, USA, USA" commenced and increased steadily in volume. It made me cry.

I was standing between Cardinal Egan and Ed Koch. As the President made his way toward us, I heard him say, "I know what I have to do." When he got to me, I shook his hand and said, "Mr. President, stay the course." He squeezed my hand, looked me right in the eye, and said, "That's exactly what I intend to do." He spoke openly and freely, although his every word was being recorded. And he meant every word he said.

For the next several weeks, I spent most of my time at Battery Park City or at the Battery Park City Command Post on Pier 92. Whenever I went down to Battery Park City, I went by way of

West Street in an official vehicle. Every time I did so, all along West Street people cheered and held up signs saying things like: THANK YOU; GOD BLESS YOU; WE LOVE YOU; USA; STAND TALL NEW YORK; and WE ARE NEW YORKERS. And all along the way, they offered water, soda, sandwiches, candy, cookies—everything under the sun. They didn't know who I was or what I was doing down there. But they knew I was involved in some way, and they just wanted to help. In my whole life, I've never witnessed such an outpouring of love, compassion, and fighting spirit. After a while, I started to take the items they were offering, not because I wanted them but because they wanted me to have them. And every time I did so, they cheered even louder. They had helped!

Our staff performed magnificently under the leadership of Tim Carey. Our Police Memorial was cleaned immediately, and the Mercantile Exchange reopened within a week, with employees commuting to work by ferryboats. Over time, water, electricity, and telephone service were restored. Our parks, gardens, streets, and sidewalks were cleaned. Air and soil quality was continuously monitored to ensure that they did not pose health hazards. Strict security was implemented to guard against looting. Buildings were cleaned by crews using state-of-the-art equipment. Buses were hired to traverse Battery Park City and connect with the subway stations and bus stops that were still operational. Damage was assessed, appropriate insurance claims were filed, and repairs and reconstruction commenced. Governor Pataki and Mayor Giuliani were spectacular in allaying fears, instilling confidence, and prevailing upon major companies such as Merrill Lynch and American Express not to abandon the World Financial Center at Battery Park City.

With the passage of time, residents, store owners, and other service providers began to return to the neighborhood. As of September of 2002, 95 percent of our residential buildings were occupied; 50 percent of the tenants of the World Financial Center were back, and almost all of our senior citizens and schoolchildren were back. We still have a way to go, but we've made extraordinary progress, and that progress continues every day.

The Ritz-Carlton, the Embassy Suites, and the Irish Hunger Memorial have opened. (The remarks I made at the opening of the Irish Hunger Memorial on July 16, 2002 are in Appendix E.)

Battery Park City on 9/11/01

Refinancing measures have been taken to ensure that our "green" building is completed as planned. Teardrop Park, in the northern neighborhood of Battery Park City, has been dedicated and is under construction. (The name Teardrop Park was chosen because of the park's shape, but the name has taken on new meaning since September 11); athletic fields have been dedicated and are under construction. In the near future, Battery Park City—indeed all of Lower Manhattan—will be better than ever!

On September 9, 2002, we added the names of the police officers killed on September 11, 2001 to the wall of honor at our Police Memorial. This is what I said on that occasion:

> Monsignor Zammit, Rabbi Kass, Governor Pataki, Mayor Bloomberg, Commissioner Kelly, family members and friends of the fallen heroes we honor today—On behalf of myself, Charles Urstadt, David Cornstein, and Tim Carey, I welcome you to our community.
>
> Five years ago, when we dedicated this sacred memorial, we said a silent prayer—that we would never have to add another name to the ones already inscribed on the wall of honor. No one could have imagined that we would gather here to add the names of 25 officers

at one time, 23 of whom were killed in the line of duty on one catastrophic day.

The most basic and fundamental—by far the strongest—instinct in humankind is the instinct for self-preservation. It prevails over all else—almost always. Those we honor today overcame that primordial instinct and gave their lives to save the lives of others. In the doing, they left behind treasured loved ones. Would you do what they did? Would I?

Only those who have been touched by a special spirit of duty and honor; only those possessed of the most powerful commitment, have it within them to make that kind of supreme sacrifice. There is no higher calling, there is no more noble virtue.

My friends, the police officers we honor today are sui generis. They are in a class by themselves. They are better than the rest of us. They are better than the wealthiest, the most powerful, the most gifted—for they are literally the best. And I know that they now are enjoying that same status in Heaven. I also know that one day you will be reunited with them.

In the meantime, please understand that this memorial does not belong to the State of New York or Battery Park City or New York City or the N.Y.P.D. It belongs to the family members and friends of those whose names are etched on the wall of honor.

I urge you to return here as often as you wish. Rest assured that this memorial will be maintained not only as a place of honor, but as a sanctuary where you can commune with your beloved fallen heroes.

Mayor Bloomberg asked me to participate in the reading of the names of those who died at Ground Zero on September 11, 2001, on the one-year anniversary of the attack on the twin towers. My partner in reading off alternate names was Ann Driscoll, whose husband was one of the police officers killed on 9/11. Although it was overwhelmingly emotional, I got through it without difficulty because I was so intent and totally focused on pronouncing each name correctly.

The United States has been attacked twice in my lifetime. The first attack came at Pearl Harbor when I was a boy. The second was directed at my own beloved New York City, in my closing years. Indeed, this recent attack struck a part of New York City for which I hold myself personally responsible. Our nation overcame the first attack by mounting the greatest war effort in the history of the world. And while it will be even more difficult this time, and will certainly take longer, we will win the war against terrorism as well. It is a *just* war, and it is one we must win if the Jameses and Gillians of this world are ever to experience the joy and comfort of a world at peace. It's about time—don't you think?

Reading the names of those who died on September 11, 2001 with Anne Driscoll.

This book began with a picture of our beloved James on the cover. It is fitting that it end with a picture of our great joy, Gillian Rose.

At Gillian's baptism by Bishop James McCarthy at St. Thomas More Church in Manhattan on February 9, 2002.

APPENDIX A

Excerpts from the speech I delivered on the occasion of Mel Glass's retirement dinner at the Fifth Avenue Hotel, February 14, 1973.

My name is Jim Gill, and I was appointed as an assistant by Mr. Hogan with our guest of honor, Mel Glass, in the summer of 1958. When we first came into the office we were assigned to the Complaint Bureau, and the chief of the bureau was Joe Stone.

After we had been in the office for about two or three months, everyone in the bureau decided that there was only one crime in the New York Penal Code, namely, false and misleading advertising. And I remember going to Joe and saying, "Joe, what about all those other crimes that I've read about in the papers—crimes like murder, rape, robbery, arson—and what about organized crime and labor racketeering and public corruption?"

He said, "Jim, you have to understand, they have us spread so thin, the most we can ever hope to do is to concentrate in the more important areas."

In those days, when you walked into Joe Stone's office it was like walking into a pawn shop. He had all sorts of things all over the floor—car batteries, radio crystal sets—but the most prominent features in Joe's room at that time were two life-size posters which were used to advertise reducing pills. The lady in the first poster weighed about 350 pounds, and over her head was the word BEFORE. The woman in the second poster was clad in a bikini. She couldn't have weighed more than a hundred pounds, and over her head were the words TWENTY-FOUR HOURS LATER.

Well, I remember when the case first came into the bureau. Joe called a bureau meeting and we studied those posters very carefully. After about three or four hours, Bob Donnelly observed, "Two hundred and fifty pounds in twenty-four hours is a lot of weight." Bob's observation triggered further study, and on the following day it was Mel Stein who noted that while both women wore tattoos, the first had hers on the left arm, whereas the second had hers on the right arm.

But the major breakthrough came on the following day—and that breakthrough was made by our guest of honor. Mel pointed out that the first woman's tattoo read MOTHER, I LOVE YOU—whereas the second woman's tattoo read DEATH BEFORE DISHONOR.

At this point, Joe Stone concluded that there was a distinct possibility that the woman in the first poster was not the same as the woman in the second poster. Joe decided to put the question to a vote of the bureau. By a vote of nine-to-eight, it was decided that the woman in the first poster was in fact the same woman as the woman in the second poster—and the case was closed.

While I voted with the majority, there is something about that case that's been nagging me ever since . . .

APPENDIX B

Excerpts from the eulogy I gave for Matty Silverman at the Yale Club, October 12, 1988.

I met Matty in the early part of 1964. He interviewed me for a job as an associate to assist him in the representation of labor unions. Many years after I was hired, I learned from Matty, to my great surprise, that he had cast the only vote against my becoming associated with our law firm.

In retrospect, it's not so surprising, because of all the odd couples in this world, we were the oddest.

I was born and raised in Waterbury, Connecticut, a factory town in the Naugatuck Valley. Matty was born and raised in New York City.

I attended a parochial grammar school, a Jesuit high school, a Jesuit College, and a Jesuit law school; Matty went through the New York City public school system, attended Amherst College, and received two degrees from Harvard University—a master's degree in history and a law degree.

I was a Marine Corps officer who loved the Marine Corps; Matty deplored the military establishment and the Marine Corps in particular.

I was a former assistant district attorney of New York County, and proud of it; Matty abhorred government prosecutors.

I was a brash, somewhat loud-mouthed Irishman; Matty was a reserved, retiring, soft-spoken Jew.

I was a practicing Catholic, and Matty was a practicing atheist.

Matty was at the far left of the political spectrum—and I was on the right.

Matty was a student of the arts; I was a student of the New York Giants football team.

And those are just some of the differences that existed between us. We made Jack Klugman and Tony Randall look like clones!

And then we began to work together and began to know each other, and all of those differences, as deep-seated as they seemed to be, started to melt away—and eventually became meaningless in terms of our relationship.

We practiced law as it ought to be practiced. We faced important and complex problems together, and we overcame them all. And we never failed to celebrate victory! More importantly, we both knew that what we were doing was worthwhile and would better the lives of human beings. Whether what we were doing was remunerative entered our minds infrequently, and when it did, it was a secondary consideration!

Matty was possessed of a brilliant legal mind and a store of legal knowledge that was awesome. In a new legal atmosphere of specialization within specialties, he was the consummate generalist. He could do it all: research the law, write a brief, try a case in any forum, and argue an appeal before any tribunal. He did it all superbly, and he did it all with gladness. Never cribbed, cabbed, or confined by subject matter or any other form of legal compartmentalization, he always envisioned the broadest legal picture with all of its legal complexities—almost a lost art today, to the detriment of the profession and those it serves.

For me, Matty's life in the law will be a continual reminder that the practice of law involves much more than "bottom-lining"—that the practice of law is not just another commercial enterprise but rather an honorable profession.

APPENDIX C

Excerpts from my speech to the Friendly Sons of St. Patrick at the Sheraton Hotel, New York City, March 17, 1992.

Last fall I traveled to Ireland for the first time. The purpose of the trip was to see Holy Cross and Fordham play football at Limerick Stadium on Saturday, November 16.

During the Aer Lingus flight I took to Shannon Airport on the Thursday before the game, the main topic of conversation was why various passengers were going to Ireland.

An English professor mused about the literary contributions of George Bernard Shaw, William Butler Yeats, James Joyce, and Sean O'Casey—and how he was looking forward to a series of lectures at Trinity College and performances at the Abbey Theater.

A young priest from Boston told us that he would be spending most of his time touring the ruins of the ancient monasteries wherein the light of Christianity was kept aglow while Europe was engulfed in barbaric darkness.

A historian regaled us with the early history of Ireland and spoke of his desire to visit the site where the great Irish warrior Brian Bórú defeated the Vikings in 1014.

Finally, the young priest from Boston said, "Mr. Gill, tell us— why are you going to Ireland?"

Rather than admit that I was going to Ireland to watch two American colleges play a game of football, I pretended to be asleep.

The next day was Friday, and I decided to drive to the Ballyvaughan, a small village on the west coast. I had been told by an old aunt that I might find relatives on the Gill side of the family if I were to visit that village.

When I reached Ballyvaughan, I went into its only pub for lunch and to make inquiries concerning my relatives. After ordering a pint of stout, I noticed that the only other customer was an elderly man who was standing at the end of the bar, talking to himself and making strange noises.

As I stared at the old man in wonderment, the bartender leaned over and whispered to me: "Pay him no mind—that's Jeremiah Gill—he's as daft as a penny watch! As a matter of fact, everyone in his family is touched."

Of course, my first thought was that there was insanity in the family and that eventually I would be institutionalized.

My dark thoughts were interrupted when the bartender asked: "By the way, what's your name?"

"I'm John Hennessey," I replied. "I'm a lawyer from New York."

At that point, I observed out of the corner of my eye—and to my horror—that Jeremiah Gill was now genuflecting in front of the bar and blessing himself with the sign of the cross over and over and over again.

"Are you here to trace some relatives?" inquired the bartender.

"Oh, no," said I, "I'm just passing through. As a matter of fact, all of my relatives are from the East Coast!"

Just then, the young priest from Boston whom I had met on the airplane the day before entered the pub and said in a loud voice, "Mr. Gill—how are you?"

I said, "I'm not Gill—I'm Hennessey."

"That's strange," replied the priest, "I could have sworn you told me your name was Gill when we met yesterday."

At that point, Jeremiah approached the priest, extended his hand, and said, "I'm Gill"—whereupon the young priest ran out of the pub.

Jeremiah then approached me, looked at me intently, and said in a low voice: "You look familiar, laddie. Tell me, do I know ye?"

"Oh, no," said I—as I started for the door. "You don't know me—and I don't know ye." And I ran out of the pub.

The next day, I went to the football game with my friend Father O'Hare.[1] While we were waiting for the game to commence, the young priest from Boston came up the aisle, spotted me, and said, "Hello, Mr. Hennessey, it's good to see you again."

---

[1] The Reverend Joseph A. O'Hare, S.J., is the president of Fordham University.

I said, "I'm not Hennessey, I'm Gill."

When the young priest was gone, Father O'Hare turned to me and said: "What was that all about?"

I said, "Father, I have no idea. I never saw that man before in my life."

That's what we who were trained by the Jesuits call a "mental reservation."

APPENDIX D

Excerpts from my introduction of Judge William Hughes Mulligan, first recipient of the St. Thomas More Award, at the Grand Hyatt Hotel, New York, September 21, 1990.

It was clear from the outset that Judge Mulligan would be a brilliant legal scholar. At the age of two months, he uttered his first words, which were: *"Res ipsa loquitur."* Two weeks later, he scrawled the words *"Quare clausum fregit"* on the floor of his playpen.

While your invitations indicate that Judge Mulligan served in counterintelligence during World War II, it makes no reference to his assignment—which was to protect the Gowanus Canal in Brooklyn against sabotage by foreign agents. Although the Gowanus Canal was blown up and totally destroyed during the war, there was no direct evidence that any of the damage was attributable to foreign agents—and accordingly Mulligan was awarded the Gowanus Canal Medal of Honor by the borough president of Brooklyn.

When the war ended, Mulligan used his distinguished military record as a springboard to become a professor at Fordham Law School, where he soon became fascinated by the law relating to attempted crimes. In an article published in the *Harvard Law Review,* he distilled this extraordinarily complicated area of the law into two simple illustrative cases: the case of the defendant who shot a tree trunk that looked like a man, and the case of the defendant who shot a man who looked like a tree trunk.

After lengthy discussion, Mulligan concluded that the defendant who shot the tree trunk was guilty of attempted murder in the first degree, whereas the defendant who shot the man had committed no crime whatever! While some were dismayed by Mulligan's conclusion, no one in the legal community could gainsay the compelling logic of his position. As a result, Mulligan was catapulted to national prominence and shortly thereafter became the dean of Fordham Law School.

The last opinion written by Judge Mulligan was in the case of *U.S. v. Byrne.* The case involved the illegal importation of swans and geese from Canada. The first paragraph of Judge Mulligan's decision reads as follows:

> Who knows what evil lurks in the hearts of men? Although the public is generally aware of the sordid trafficking of drugs and aliens across our borders, this litigation alerts us to a nefarious practice hitherto unsuspected even by this rather calloused bench: rare-bird smuggling. While Canadian geese have been regularly crossing, exiting, reentering, and departing our borders with impunity, and apparently without documentation, to enjoy more salubrious climes, those unwilling or unable to make the flight—either because of inadequate wingspan, lack of fuel, or fear of buckshot— have become prey to unscrupulous traffickers who put them in crates and ship them to American ports of entry with fraudulent documentation—in violation of a host of federal statutes. The traffic has been egregious enough to warrant the empaneling of a special grand jury in the Northern District of New York. Even the services of the Royal Canadian Mounted Police were mustered to aid the inquiry.

The last sentence of Mulligan's opinion reads: "The judgment of conviction is affirmed, justice has triumphed, and this is my swan song."

I attended Fordham Law School from 1953 to 1956, and during that time I took every course that Professor Mulligan taught. And I can tell you that he was the brightest, the most enlightening, the most inspiring, and the most entertaining teacher that ever stood in front of a classroom.

As dean, he brought our law school to Lincoln Center and to national prominence. No one has done more for our law school than Dean Mulligan.

The many opinions that Judge Mulligan authored while serving on the Second Circuit Court of Appeals will be a valued legacy for lawyers and judges for generations to come. And his speeches will be a joy forever.

Judge Mulligan is a man of varied and enormous talents. He is a man of unflinching and uncompromising integrity. He is a man of great courage and unswerving loyalty. He is universally admired and respected, and he is universally loved. It is most fitting that he is the first recipient of the St. Thomas More Award.

APPENDIX E

Speech I gave at the Opening of the Irish Hunger Memorial at Battery Park City, July 16, 2002

Your Eminence Cardinal Egan, President McAleese, Governor Pataki, Mayor Bloomberg, Speaker Silver, members of the diplomatic corps, distinguished members of the executive committee, honored guests, my fellow New Yorkers.

During the Irish Hunger of 1845 to 1852, more than one million people died of starvation and hunger-related diseases. More than two million were forced to leave their native country. Ireland, in her most desperate hour of need, sent forth the seeds of her own deliverance. Irish men, women, and children, risking death in what were referred to as "coffin ships," bravely traveled to the corners of the earth, bringing with them a willingness to work and a determination to be free.

It would be impossible to overstate the importance of Irish immigration to the City and State of New York. Between 1847 and 1851, more than 848,000 Irish immigrants arrived in New York City alone, many of them landing on the piers and docks that used to be located where we are now gathered. The Irish who came to America produced government leaders, orators, poets and playwrights, historians, scholars, actors, leaders of the Church, captains of commercial enterprise, as well as police officers, firefighters, and rescue workers such as those who gave their lives in the attack upon America which took place two blocks away on September 11. The next time the names of those who sacrificed their lives in that tragedy are listed, I would ask you to read those names and you will see what I mean.

Undoubtedly the saddest aspect of the Irish Hunger is that it need not have happened. At that time the European economy was soaring, and the prime beneficiary of that economy was England. There were ample funds in England for famine relief. But there were also voices in London proclaiming the potato blight to be the result of "Divine Providence"; that God was punishing the Irish for laziness and "popery." Not even the potato itself was safe from this calumny. It was said that the potato was the vegetable of the lazy because it grew virtually anywhere and required little preparation for consumption. And so the hunger was met with studied indifference.

But while we must never forget the Irish Hunger, we must never dwell upon it with a view towards perpetual hatred. There is not an English person alive who participated in the gross indifference that was at the core of the Irish Hunger. Nor is there a sensible English person alive who would condone it.

The aspect of this Memorial that I savor most is that it is truly a living Memorial. The landscaping is authentically Irish, and will remain so. More than 60 species of Irish plants and grasses have taken root in this Memorial. There are stones throughout the Memorial from every county in Ireland, symbolizing a united Ireland of 32 counties.

The text on the sides of the Memorial sets forth quotes, newspaper reports, poetry, and literature, which are changeable and will be replaced periodically. Soon there will be a World Hunger Library housed next to the Memorial, containing books, writings, and reports concerning the Irish Hunger. Finally and most importantly, the Memorial will be equipped with audio messages that will bring immediate attention to starvation wherever or whenever it occurs throughout the world. In conjunction with the United Nations, we will work to assist in the immediate distribution of food to those areas.

Ladies and gentlemen, the wonderful Memorial before us today is not just another "man on a horse." It is a very special achievement, and needless to say we are enormously proud of it.

A great deal of credit is owed to a great number of people in connection with this Memorial. I thank Governor Pataki, Mayor Bloomberg, Speaker Silver, my fellow Board members Charlie Urstadt and David Cornstein, the members of our executive committee, our president and chief executive officer Tim Carey, and our magnificent staff. But most of all I would single out for special credit our extremely talented artist, Brian Tolle, and the skilled workers who actually built this Memorial with their bare hands and with incredible and unstinting devotion and creativity.

I thank each and every one of you and I hope that you will derive satisfaction in the knowledge that a part of you is in this Memorial.

INDEX

Page numbers in italics indicate photograph.